First published and printed in 2005 by
The Orcadian Limited, Hatston, Kirkwall Orkney

ISBN 1-902957-24-5

# Sillocks, Skarfies & Selkies

The Vertebrate Fauna of

## - ORKNEY -

by

Chris & Jean Booth

# Foreword

There are questions about some of Orkney's wildlife that are often asked, such as : Does it occur in Orkney? When and where can it be seen? Is it rare?

The purpose of this book is to try, if possible, to answer some of these questions by documenting, where relevant, the past history and, more importantly, what is known about an animal's present status. However, as populations are continually changing, once published, the information may already be out of date. Details of subsequent records will be found in future editions of the annually published Orkney Field Club Bulletin and Orkney Bird Report.

The first attempt at a complete list was Buckley and Harvie-Brown's *A Vertebrate Fauna of the Orkney Islands* in 1891, this book has been the source of much historical information. It was followed, just over 100 years later, by the *Status and Checklist of the Vertebrate Fauna of Orkney* published in 1998.

To aid identification of the mammals a brief description has been included. Bird identification is well covered in the many Field Guides that are available.

Unless otherwise stated the species summaries are based on records up to the end of 2004. Sources of more detailed information are given in the references.

Where known, local names of species are given in brackets.

Harrabrough, Herston, St Margaret's Hope - Photo ©Drew Kennedy

# Acknowledgements



This book would not have been possible but for the efforts of many observers who, over the years, have contributed records of their sightings. To all of them we are extremely grateful.

We are also greatly indebted to the following whose photographs illustrate this book: Leonard Bain, Ross Flett, Edwin Groat, Ian Hourston, Bob Inkster, Keith Johnson, Drew Kennedy, Peter & Viv Reynolds, Gil Steven, Colin Thomson, Malcolm Thomson, Rod Thorne, Dennis & Sheila Walls and Stuart Williams.

Our thanks to Keith Johnson for information on Orkney's weather, to James Miller for his encouragement to compile this book and especially to Drew Kennedy whose hard work has brought everything together.

Chris & Jean Booth

Observers' records are always welcome.

If possible these should be sent to the relevant recorder, otherwise to Chris Booth - Tel. 01856 872883, E-mail: BoothRonas@aol.com or Orkney Biodiversity Records Centre, c/o Orkney Library, Kirkwall - Tel. 01856 873166, E-mail: biodiversity@orkney.gov.uk

Risso's Dolphins - Holm - Photo ©Drew Kennedy

# Map of Orkney

# Introduction



Situated off the north east tip of Scotland and separated from it by the waters of the Pentland Firth, Orkney consists of a group of around 70 islands, with a total land area of approximately 1,000 sq.km. At least 19 of the islands are inhabited. The nearest point of the Scottish mainland, Duncansby Head in Caithness, is just 10km from the south west tip of South Ronaldsay.

Orcinus Orca- Photo ©Bob Inkster

The islands are composed principally of rocks of the Old Red Sandstone series, presenting a landscape of mainly low rounded hills and fertile soils. The island of Hoy is more spectacular with higher hills and deep glacial valleys, here the Ward Hill rises to 479 metres and there are nine other summits over 300m. Elsewhere the highest points are 268m on Mainland and 250m on Rousay.

Orkney's habitats are diverse and include sub-arctic fellfield, moorland, rough grassland, marsh, freshwater lochs and agricultural crops, such as reseeded grassland and cereals. Open habitats dominate and native woodland is confined to one surviving fragment on Hoy. There are several well established, but generally small, plantations (coniferous and deciduous) and further tree planting is taking place on a number of islands. Both rocky and soft shores, including sand dunes and associated machair, are to be found on the 800 kilometres of Orkney's coastline.

Orkney Vole - Photo ©P & V Reynolds

The climate can be described as "equable maritime" which experiences many and varied changes, even in a single day. The islands are heavily influenced by the surrounding sea which has a temperature range of 7.5°C at its coldest in March/April and 14.5°C at its warmest in August. These temperatures

# Introduction cont.

appear modest but are the sole reason why Orkney experiences little frost and few sub zero temperatures in winter. The annual mean maximum temperature is 10.1°C (January is lowest at 5.5°C and August highest at 15.4°C) and the annual mean minimum temperature is 5.4°C (February is lowest at 1.6°C and August highest at 9.9°C). These averages are over the period 1950-2000, however, over the past 5 years the mean maximum has been 11.3°C. The relative humidity rarely falls below 70%, while the annual rainfall is just under 1 metre. The number of gale days per annum has ranged between 7 and 54 over a 55 year period.

Humans have lived on Orkney for at least 5,000 years and their presence has greatly affected the environment. There have been many changes just within the last 100 years, particularly in fishing and farming methods, as well as in land use. All these have had an influence on Orkney's wildlife and there will be further changes.

Ring of Brodgar, Stenness - Photo ©Drew Kennedy

# Contents

Raven - Photo - Chris Booth

# Fish

The recording of fish in Orkney waters, and publication of information on their status, was somewhat neglected for most of the 20th century. In 1997 Prof. Jonathan Side of ICIT, Heriot-Watt University, Orkney, started collating, from a number of sources, all available fish records for Orkney. As part of the Orkney Science Festival in September 1998, Prof. Side presented a paper on Orkney Fishes to a working group on Orkney's Marine Biodiversity. The following list is based on this paper with additional records that have been collected in subsequent years.

Our knowledge of the occurrence, distribution and population sizes of different fish varies considerably. For a number of species the status given must be considered to be provisional. When more data is available it may be possible, for some species at least, to make a more accurate statement.

The records used in the list are for fish reported within approximately 30 nautical miles of the Orkney coast. The order of species follows that given in *A List of the Common Scientific Names of Fishes of the British Isles* by Alwyne Wheeler (1992) published in The Journal of Fish Biology, 41 Supplement A.

Off Copinsay ©Drew Kennedy

# Fish

## LAMPREYS : Petromyzontidae

**SEA LAMPREY** *Petromyzon marinus* — Very rare

There are 2 records in the 19th century, but no recent records.

## RAT-FISHES : Chimaeridae

**RABBIT-FISH or Rat Fish** *Chimaera monstrosa* — Frequent

Probably common in deep water off-shore to the north and west. 1 record in the 19th century.

## MACKEREL SHARKS : Lamnidae

**PORBEAGLE** *Lamna nasus* — Probably fairly common

Caught fairly regularly off Sanday and there are also recent reports from Scapa Flow and off Hoy. Most records are between September and December, with the majority in November.

**BASKING SHARK (Homer)** *Cetorhinus maximus* — Fairly common

There are 1 or 2 reports during most years but this species would appear to be less frequent now, than in the early part of the 20th century. Recorded between May and December, but with most sightings in August and September.

**THRESHER SHARK** *Alopias vulpinus* — Rare in Orkney coastal waters

The only recent record is of 1 stranded at Dingieshowe, Deerness on 27th May 1967. It was 3.89m in length.

## DOGFISHES : Scyliorhinidae

**LESSER SPOTTED DOGFISH, Dogfish or Sandy Dogfish**
*Scyliorhinus canicula* — Frequent if not common

Sometimes found in creels and occasionally caught by anglers when boat or shore fishing.

**NURSEHOUND or Greater Spotted Dogfish** *Scyliorhinus stellaris* — Rare

May be confused with the previous species.

## REQUIEM SHARKS AND SMOOTH HOUNDS : Carcharhinidae

**BLUE SHARK** *Prionace glauca* — Infrequent

Towards the limit of its geographical range. Most recent records are a sighting in 1955 and at least 9 strandings of dead sharks since 1990, they had lengths of between 1.5 and 2.11m.

**TOPE** *Galeorhinus galeus* — Infrequent

1 record in the 19th century. Movements are not fully known but this species probably occurs regularly in coastal waters in August. During the 2003 International Sea Angling Festival 2 were caught off Skaill, Sandwick in the first week of August, while several were trapped in a net in the mouth of Otterswick, Sanday on 11th August 2003.

**STARRY SMOOTH HOUND** *Mustelus asterias* — Probably very rare

1 was caught in a trawl in 1990.

**SMOOTH HOUND** *Mustelus mustelus* — Rare

No recent records.

## SPINY SHARKS : Squalidae

**SPURDOG (Hoe)** *Squalus acanthias* — Infrequent inshore, Common offshore

Occasionally caught by anglers while boat fishing.

**GREENLAND SHARK** *Somniosus microcephalus* Rare
At the southern limit of its geographical range. Recorded in 19th century.

## ANGEL SHARKS : Squatinidae

**MONKFISH or Angel Shark** *Squatina squatina* Rare
At the limit of its geographical range. In the 20th century there were 2 records, in 1912 and 1972.

## ELECTRIC RAYS : Torpedinidae

**ELECTRIC RAY** *Torpedo nobiliana* Rare
At the northern limit of its range. 1 was caught in a seine net on 8th September 1987, it weighed 28kg.

## SKATES AND RAYS : Rajidae

**WHITE SKATE** *Raja alba* Record uncertain
A 19th century record which now is not possible to confirm.

**SKATE** *Raja batis* Frequent, but less so than formerly
Can reach a large size, with some fish weighing over 68 kgm.

**BLONDE RAY** *Raja brachyura* Rare
Towards the limit of its normal range. The only record is of 1 taken in a trawl in 1996.

**THORNBACK RAY or Roker** *Raja clavata* Common
Probably the commonest of the rays found in inshore coastal waters.

**PALE RAY** *Raja lintea* Rare
1 record in the 19th century. Beyond the southern limit of its geographical range.

**SPOTTED RAY or Homelyn Ray** *Raja montagui* Rare
At the northern limit of its range. Recorded in surveys and trawls in Orkney waters. 1 weighing 2.72kg was caught off Hatston Pier on 19th March 2005.

**CUCKOO RAY** *Raja naevus* Rare
Towards the northern limit of its range. Has been recorded on several occasions in recent years.

**BLACK SKATE** *Raja nidarosiensis* Rare
The only records are of egg cases found on the shore.

**STARRY RAY** Raja radiata Rare in inshore waters
Common in deeper waters to the north.

## STURGEONS : Acipenseridae

**STURGEON** *Acipenser sturio* Very rare
1, weighing approximately 315 kgms, was caught off the east coast of Westray in October 1956.

## EEL : Anguillidae

**EEL** *Anguilla anguilla* Common and locally abundant
Found in both freshwater and marine habitats.

# Fish

## CONGER EEL : Congridae

**CONGER EEL** *Conger conger* Well distributed around the coast. Common

## HERRINGS : Clupeidae

**ALLIS SHAD** *Alosa alosa* Rare

The only record is of a male caught in a seine net on 16th February 1990. It is not known to have spawned in Orkney burns.

**HERRING** *Clupea harengus* Common but less so than previously

Only the young are common in inshore waters.

**PILCHARD or Sardine** *Sardinia pichardus* Rare

1 record from a trawl in 1996. This species is at the northern limit of its range, but numbers were reported to be present in Orkney waters in 2003.

**SPRAT** *Sprattus sprattus* Common

Although there are few actual records, probably spawns in Orkney waters. It is an abundant fish in northern European waters.

## ANCHOVIES : Engraulidae

**ANCHOVY** *Engraulis encrasicolus* Rare

At the limit of its geographical range. 1 record in the 19th century. Numbers were reported to have been caught in Orkney waters in 2003.

## CARP : Cyprinidae

Photo ©Malcolm Thomson

**MINNOW** *Phoxinus phoxinus* Introduced

It is not known when this fish was introduced. A shoal of about 200 was seen in the Loch of Boardhouse on 6th July 2003, several had the colouration of breeding males. Its presence in the connecting complex of lochs and burns was confirmed when 1 was caught in the Burn of Hillside on 13th July 2003. Minnows have also been found in the outflow burn from Loch of Swannay.

## LOACHES : Cobitidae

Photo ©Chris Booth

**STONE LOACH** *Barbatula barbatulus* Introduced

First discovered in 1988 in the Burn of Hillside in the West Mainland but was not actually recorded until 1990, when it was also found in the Burn of Lushan. It was reported from the Loch of Hundland in 1997 and the Loch of Boardhouse in 1999.

## ARGENTINES : Argentinidae

**GREATER ARGENTINE** *Argentina silus* Infrequent

More abundant in deeper offshore waters.

**ARGENTINE** *Argentina sphyraena* Infrequent

Infrequent in inshore waters.

## SMELTS : Osmeridae

**SMELT or Sparling** *Osmerus eperlanus* Rare

There is a 19th century record from Watersound. Occasionally recorded in commercial catches in waters adjacent to Orkney.

## SALMON FISHES : Salmonidae

**RAINBOW TROUT** *Oncorhynchus mykiss* — **Introduced, extinct**
There have been several unsuccessful attempts, both on Mainland and the North Isles, to introduce this species.

**SALMON** *Salmo salar* — Rare in its wild form
Occasionally runs up 1 or 2 of the larger burns and is sometimes caught by anglers while shore fishing.

**TROUT, Sea Trout or Brown Trout** — Common
*Salmo trutta*
Common and well distributed in lochs and burns, but less so in its wild form than previously. It has been introduced into lochs in the North Isles.

Photo Chris Booth

**CHARR or Arctic Charr** *Salvelinus alpinus* — **Extinct**
Formerly found in Heldale Water, Hoy. 1 caught in 2003 was probably a reintroduction of a locally reared fish.

## COD FISHES : Gadidae

**TORSK** *Brosme brosme* — Common offshore in deeper waters
Occasionally caught by sea anglers.

**FIVE-BEARDED ROCKLING** *Ciliata mustela* — Abundant
Widespread on Orkney shores throughout the year.

**SILVERY POUT** *Gadiculus argenteus thori* — Frequent in deeper water
Frequent in deep water to the west and north. Several taken during a trawl in 1996.

**COD** *Gadus morhua* — Common
Common around the islands and especially offshore.

**SHORE ROCKLING** *Gaidropsarus mediterraneus* — Uncommon
At the north of its range. There are recent records from Birsay, Deerness and South Ronaldsay.

**THREE-BEARDED ROCKLING (Slapper)** *Gaidropsarus vulgaris* — Frequent
Often captured in creels.

**HADDOCK** *Melanogrammus aeglefinus* — Common offshore
Sporadic in inshore waters.

**WHITING** *Merlangius merlangus* — Common, especially offshore
Many records.

**BLUE LING** *Molva dipterygia* — Frequent in deeper waters offshore
At the south of its range. The only records are from commercial catches.

**LING** *Molva molva* — Common
Found in large numbers around wrecks, often caught by boat anglers.

**GREATER FORK-BEARD** *Phycis blennoides* — Infrequent
Mostly found in deeper offshore waters.

**POLLACK or Lythe (Sillock, Cuithe)** *Pollachius pollachius* — Common
Common around rocky shores, especially during late summer.

# Fish

**COALFISH or Saithe, (Sillock, Cuithe)** *Pollachius virens* — Common
Common and often abundant in coastal waters, particularly during its early years.

**NORWAY POUT** *Trisopterus esmarki* — Common offshore
Often taken in commercial fishery.

**BIB or Pouting** *Trisopterus luscus* — Probably uncommon
Only a few records.

**POOR-COD (Red Ware Cod)** *Trisopterus minutus* — Common
Often taken in creels. May be abundant in some inshore areas.

## TADPOLE-FISH : Ranicipiteridae

Photo ©Chris Booth

**TADPOLE-FISH** *Raniceps raninus* — Fairly common
Sometimes found on shore after gales, also caught in lobster creels.

## HAKES : Merlucciidae

**HAKE** *Merluccius merluccius* — Common offshore
Mostly found in deeper waters.

## RAT-TAILS : Macrouridae

**ROUNDHEAD RAT-TAIL/ROUNDNOSE GRENADIER** *Coryphaenoides rupestris* — Common in deeper waters offshore
Occasionally found in commercial catches.

## ANGLER FISHES : Lophiidae

**ANGLER (Monk, Mersgam or Fishing frog)** *Lophius piscatorius* — Common
Regularly taken in commercial catches and sometimes found stranded on shore after gales.

## CLINGFISHES : Gobiesocidae

**SMALL-HEADED CLINGFISH** *Apletodon dentatus* — Rare
At the limit of its geographical range. There are 2 records, of single fish, in 1996 and 1997.

**TWO-SPOTTED CLINGFISH** *Diplecogaster bimaculata* — Occasional
Found in inshore waters, the commonest of the clingfishes in Orkney.

**CONNEMARA CLINGFISH** *Lepadogaster candollei* — Rare
At the limit of its geographical range. 1 record in September 1962.

**SHORE CLINGFISH** *Lepadogaster lepadogaster* — Rare
At the limit of its geographical range. 1 in 1850, and a male and female found in Birsay Bay on 9th April 2001

## GARFISH : Belonidae

Photo ©Chris Booth

**GARFISH** *Belone belone* — Infrequent
Stranded specimens recorded on a number of occasions since 1953.

## SKIPPER : Scomberesocidae

**SKIPPER** *Scomberesox saurus* — Infrequent
Sometimes occurs in large numbers.

## OPAH : Lampridae

**OPAH** *Lampris guttatus* — Infrequent

An oceanic fish, most recent records are in August 1976, November 1982 and October 1995.

## DEAL-FISH : Trachipteridae

**DEAL-FISH** *Trachipterus arcticus* — Infrequent offshore

There have been 4 reported strandings since 1964.

## OAR-FISH : Regalecidae

**OAR-FISH or Ribbon-Fish** *Regalecus glesne* — Rare

A single 19th century record and 1 in 1936, both strandings.

## DORY : Zeidae

**DORY or John Dory** *Zeus faber* — Uncommon, if not rare

At the northern limit of its range; 4 recent records in 1968, 1970, 1996 (2).

Photo ©Chris Booth

## BOAR-FISH : Caproidae

**BOAR-FISH** *Capros aper* — Rare

A fish of deeper water where it may be common. The only records are of 2 caught in a trawl off the east side of Orkney in May 1990 and 1 found dead at Dingieshowe, Deerness on 4th November 2003.

Photo ©Chris Booth

## STICKLEBACKS : Gasterosteidae

**THREE-SPINED STICKLEBACK or Stickleback** *Gasterosteus aculeatus* — Common and locally abundant

Common in freshwater, brackish water and, particularly, in marine habitats.

**FIFTEEN-SPINED STICKLEBACK or Sea Stickleback** *Spinachia spinachia* — Common and locally abundant

Common in rock pools; not found in freshwater.

## PIPEFISHES : Syngnathidae

**SNAKE PIPEFISH** *Entelurus aequorius* — Uncommon

Uncommon in inshore waters. There are 10 records since 1956.

**SHORT-SNOUTED SEAHORSE** *Hippocampus hippocampus* — Record uncertain

1 found dead in 1853. There is some doubt as to whether the record should refer to *Hippocampus ramulosus* (seahorse) rather than *H. hippocampus*. It has also been suggested that it was a sailor's discarded trinket.

**WORM PIPEFISH** *Nerophis lumbriciformis* — Uncommon

Recent records are from rock pools and the tidal zone.

**GREATER PIPEFISH** *Syngnathus acus* — Infrequent

Locally abundant on Zostera beds.

**NILSSON'S PIPEFISH** *Syngnathus rostellatus* Rare
Probably at the northern limit of its geographical range. The only record is of a male and 2 females in Widewall Bay, South Ronaldsay on 14th August 1998.

**DEEP-SNOUTED PIPEFISH** *Syngnathus typhle* Rare
Only 19th century records.

## SCORPION - AND RED-FISHES : Scorpaenidae

**BLUE-MOUTH** *Helicolenus dactylopterus* Rare inshore
A deep water fish. Occasionally occurring in commercial catches.

**RED SCORPION-FISH** *Scorpaena scrofa* Very rare
Common in the western Mediterranean but very rare in northern European waters. The only record is of 1 observed by a diver.

**RED-FISH** *Sebastes norvegicus* Rare inshore
Abundant in northern offshore waters.

**NORWAY HADDOCK** *Sebastes viviparus* Infrequent
Occasionally caught by boat anglers, the most recent was off Hoy in July 1997. Common offshore in deeper waters.

## GURNARDS : Triglidae

**RED GURNARD** *Aspitrigla cuculus* Rare
1 from the Pentland Firth in 1965 is the most recent record. At the limit of its range. Sometimes found in commercial catches.

**GREY GURNARD** *Eutrigla gurnardus* Infrequent
The most common of the gurnards in Orkney waters. 1 was caught off South Ronaldsay in 1971; is also found in some commercial catches..

**TUB GURNARD** *Trigla lucerna* Rare
1 record, a diver observation off Orphir in July 1997.

## BULLHEADS : Cottidae

**BULL-ROUT or Short-spined Sea Scorpion** *Myoxocephalus scorpius* Common
Locally abundant, frequently caught in creels.

**SEA SCORPION (Comper)** Taurulus bubalis Common
Locally abundant, young fish frequently found in rock pools during the summer months.

## POGGES : Agonidae

**HOOK-NOSE, Pogge or Armed Bullhead** *Agonus cataphractus* Uncommon
Occasionally taken in creels.

## LUMPSUCKER : Cyclopteridae

**LUMPSUCKER** *Cyclopterus lumpus* Common
Often taken in creels and occasionally stranded.

## SEA-SNAILS : Liparidae

**SEA-SNAIL** *Liparis liparis* Probably very rare
Stated to be common in the 19th century but recent searches have failed to find any. There may have been confusion with Montagu's sea snail

**MONTAGU'S SEA-SNAIL** *Liparis montagui* Uncommon
Most often found on the shore at very low tides.

## SEA BASSES : Percichthyidae

**BASS** *Dicentrarchus labrax* Uncommon
Only recorded in recent years; single specimens in 1965 and 1972, then since 1992 several have been caught by anglers fishing from the shore. 1 weighing 2.7kgs was caught in a creel off Sanday on 24th November, 2004.

## HORSE MACKERELS : Carangidae

**SCAD or Horse mackerel** *Trachurus trachurus* Common offshore
Infrequent inshore, 1 caught off Rousay in September 1963.

## RAY'S BREAM : Bramidae

**RAY'S BREAM** *Brama brama* Uncommon inshore
13 records of strandings since 1923. Seasonally frequent offshore.

## SEA-BREAMS : Sparidae

**RED SEA-BREAM** *Pagellus bogaraveo* Rare, at least recently
Only 19th century records. At the northern limit of its range.

**GILTHEAD** *Sparus aurata* Rare
Only recent record is of 1 caught in the Pentland Firth in 1992.

**BLACK SEA-BREAM** *Spondyliosoma cantharus* Rare
1 caught northwest of Hoy in Feb. 1965 is the only record. At the limit of its geographical range.

## SHADE-FISHES : Sciaenidae

**MEAGRE** *Argyrosomus regius* Very rare
1 record in 1856, very rare in northern European waters.

## RED MULLETS : Mullidae

**RED MULLET** *Mullus surmuletus* Rare
4 were seen by a diver off No 4 Barrier in August 1976, has also recently been recorded by Orkney Harbour Authority Environmental Unit.

## GREY MULLETS : Mugilidae

**THICK-LIPPED GREY MULLET** *Chelon labrosus* Uncommon
Single fish caught at Skaill, Sandwick in 1955 and 1964, also 1 ashore in Burray in 1964. 1 seen in Deerness in 1971 and more recently small schools have been reported from Quindry, South Ronaldsay in August.

## WRASSES : Labridae

**ROCK-COOK** *Centrolabrus exoletus* Rare
The only recent record is of a diver observation in Scapa Flow in 1997.

**CORKWING WRASSE** *Crenilabrus melops* Rare
There is a record of a specimen from Stromness in June 1963.

**GOLDSINNY** *Ctenolabrus rupestris* Probably rare
Single records in 1962 and 1965, also 2 diver observations in 1997.

**BALLAN WRASSE** *Labrus bergylta* — Common, locally abundant
Abundant about wrecks and steep underwater cliffs, often caught by shore anglers.

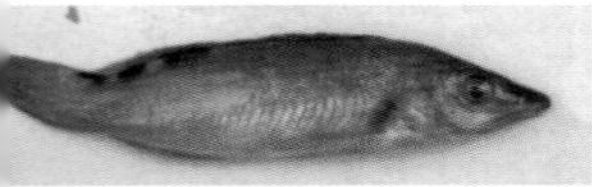
Photo ©Chris Booth

**CUCKOO WRASSE** *Labrus mixtus* — Locally common
There are widespread records from throughout the islands, migrates into deeper water in early winter.

## EELPOUTS : Zoarcidae

**EELPOUT or Viviparous Blenny (Greenbanes)** *Zoarces viviparus* — Abundant
One of the commonest fishes of the shore, found under rocks and stones in rock pools.

## ARCTIC BLENNIES : Stichaeidae

**YARRELL'S BLENNY** *Chirolophis ascanii* — Infrequent
Said to be common in the 19th century but possibly only locally common at times. Recent diver observations from Scapa Flow and Papa Westray.

## BUTTERFISH : Pholidae

**BUTTERFISH or Gunnel (Swordick, Swordo or Razorfish)** *Pholis gunnellus* — Abundant
A common fish of the shore and shallow coastal waters.

## WOLF-FISHES : Anarhichadidae

**WOLF-FISH or Cat-Fish** *Anarhichas lupus* — Common offshore
Occasionally stranded after storms; 1 was found on the shore in Sanday in 1982. Taken regularly in commercial catches.

## WEEVERS : Trachinidae

**WEEVER or Lesser Weever** *Echiichthys vipera* — Probably uncommon
At the northern limit of its geographical range. There were 6 records between 1963 and 1998. In 1999, 15 were caught at 4 different sites, in beach seine hauls, from 8th July to 17th September.

**GREATER WEEVER** *Trachinus draco* — Rare
At the northern limit of its geographical range, usually found in deeper water than previous species. There are 2 records, 1 at Scapa in 1897 and the other caught in a beach seine haul at the Sands of Wright, South Ronaldsay on 10th August 1999.

## BLENNIES : Blenniidae

**BUTTERFLY BLENNY** *Blennius ocellaris* — Rare
There is a single record of 1 taken in 1849. It is rare to the north of the Irish Sea.

**SHANNY** *Lipophrys pholis* — Abundant
Probably the commonest fish of the Orkney shore in recent years. There are no 19th century records. First reported in 1958, when it was considered to be fairly common around Stromness.

## SANDEELS : Ammodytidae

**RAITT'S SANDEEL** *Ammodytes marinus* — Common offshore
1 was found in Holm, March 1962.

**SANDEEL** *Ammodytes tobianus* — Common
A very common inshore fish, but there may have been a recent decline.

**GREATER SANDEEL or Launce** *Hyperoplus lanceolatus* Probably uncommon
There have been 4 records since 1955.

## DRAGONETS : Callionymidae

**DRAGONET** *Callionymus lyra* Common
Common over sandy and muddy areas of the sea bottom.

**SPOTTED DRAGONET** *Callionymus maculatus* Uncommon
Uncommon in coastal waters. The only records are from trawls in 1996.

**RETICULATED DRAGONET** *Callionymus reticulatus* Probably rare
1 diver record in 1997; possibly at the edge of its geographical range.

## GOBIES : Gobiidae

**BLACK GOBY** *Gobius niger* Rare
Recorded in 19th century, but despite recent searches, there are no 20th century records.

**TWO-SPOTTED GOBY** *Gobiusculus flavescens* Locally common
Only recently recorded, found in Zostera beds in Orkney.

**COMMON GOBY** *Pomatoschistus microps* Probably rare
Just 1 record, a diver observation in 1997.

**SAND GOBY** *Pomatoschistus minutus* Perhaps locally common
The most recent records are in 1997 and 1998

**PAINTED GOBY** *Pomatoschistus pictus* Perhaps locally common
First noted in August 1964, has since been recorded on a number of occasions.

**LEOPARD-SPOTTED GOBY** *Thorogobius ephippiatus* Probably rare
The only record is of a diver observation in 1997.

## SCABBARDFISHES : Trichiuridae

**SCABBARDFISH** *Lepidopus caudatus* Uncommon
The only records are from commercial catches in adjacent waters. At the edge of its geographical range.

## MACKERELS AND TUNNIES : Scombridae

**MACKEREL** *Scomber scombrus* Sometimes abundant
Abundant in some years when on migratory passage and almost absent in others; probably commonest in July and August.

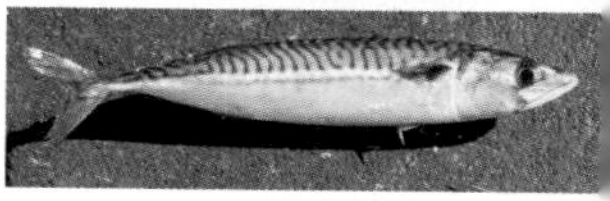

Photo ©Drew Kennedy

**LONG-FIN TUNNY or Albacore** *Thunnus alalunga* Record uncertain
A tunny, thought to have been of this species, weighing about 20 kgms, was caught off Orkney in 1900.

**BLUE-FIN TUNNY** *Thunnus thynnus* Rare
There are 4 records, the most recent being of 1 washed ashore on Papa Westray in January 1955 and bones found on Papa Stronsay in March 1964.

## SWORDFISH : Xiphiidae

**SWORDFISH** *Xiphias gladius* — Records uncertain
Recorded in the 19th century. Some early records must be treated with caution as the name "Swordfish" was sometimes used by fishermen to describe male Killer whales with a tall dorsal fin. No recent records.

## LEFT-EYED FLATFISHES : Scophthalmidae

**MEGRIM** *Lepidorhombus whiffiagonis* — Common offshore
Often abundant in commercial catches in deeper water adjacent to the coast.

**NORWEGIAN TOPKNOT** *Phrynorhombus norvegicus* — Perhaps uncommon
A difficult fish to capture and observe. There is 1 diver record, in 1997.

**ECKSTROM'S TOPKNOT** *Phrynorhombus regius* — Probably very rare
1 caught in July 1997 may be the most northerly record of this fish. Orkney is beyond the limit of its known geographical range.

**TURBOT** *Scophthalmus maximus* — Uncommon
There are several records since 1976 including small numbers of juveniles found in suitable sandy bays.

**BRILL (Quirnfish)** *Scophthalmus rhombus* — Uncommon
Close to the edge of its geographical range.

**TOPKNOT** *Zeugopterus punctatus* — Possibly common in suitable localities
Said to be common at Swanbister, Orphir in 19th century. There are 3 dated 20th century records and 1 was caught at Otterswick, Sanday on 22nd August 2000.

## RIGHT-EYED FLATFISHES : Pleuronectidae

**WITCH** *Glyptocephalus cynoglossus* — Common offshore
Only recorded from deep water trawls and commercial catches.

**LONG ROUGH DAB** *Hippoglossoides platessoides* — Common offshore
No coastal records.

**HALIBUT** *Hippoglossus hippoglossus* — Fairly common in deeper offshore waters
Not as common as in the 19th century. This species is now only rarely taken by boat anglers. 1 weighing 72 kgms was caught off Marwick in 1968.

**DAB** *Limanda limanda* — Common offshore
Less common in coastal waters.

**LEMON SOLE** *Microstomus kitt* — Locally common offshore
Does not appear to be found in inshore coastal waters.

**FLOUNDER** *Pleuronectes flesus* — Common
Widespread around the coast where there are freshwater inflows.

**PLAICE** *Pleuronectes platessa* — Common
Locally abundant in some sandy bays when young.

**GREENLAND HALIBUT** *Reinhardius hippoglossoides* — Rare
A deep water fish, at the edge of its range. There are records of catches in sea areas adjacent to the Orkney coasts.

## SOLES : Soleidae

**SOLENETTE** *Buglossidium luteum* Rare
1 record of a fish taken in a trawl. At the northern limit of its range.

**SAND SOLE** *Solea lascaris* Very rare
1 record in the 19th century. A rare fish in northern European waters

**SOLE** *Solea solea* Uncommon
Probably an occasional visitor, only a few records.

## TRIGGERFISH : Balistidae

**TRIGGERFISH** *Balistes capriscus* Rare
A 19th century record. There were 2 records in September 1995, 2 in 1997 (October and November), 1 in September 2001 and 1 in September 2004.

Photo ©Chris Booth

## PUFFERFISH : Tetraodontidae

**PUFFERFISH** *Lagocephalus lagocephalus* Rare
There were 2 records in the 19th century.

## SUNFISHES : Molidae

**SUNFISH** *Mola mola* Uncommon vagrant
There have been at least 9 records since 1990 involving both live and dead fish.

**TRUNCATED SUNFISH** *Ranzania laevis* Very rare
1 record in November 1875.

# Amphibians

There is very little information given by early writers on the status of amphibians in the islands but it is probable that their presence in Orkney is due to human introductions. Recent interest in creating garden ponds means that introductions continue.

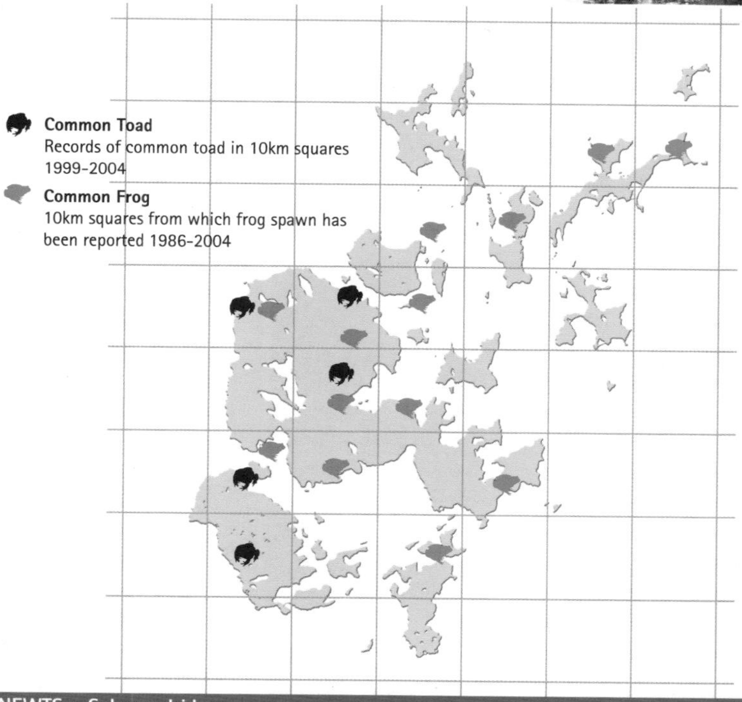


## NEWTS : Salamandridae

### NEWT *Triturus sp.*

Introduced, rare

There have been several attempts to introduce newts, probably either Smooth *Triturus vulgaris* or Palmate *Triturus helveticus*, over the years. Most recent attempts were in Toab, East Mainland in 1985 and 1987, when several adults were released. On South Ronaldsay a number of Smooth newts was released between 1982 and 1987 and 6 Palmate newts in about 1988. There were sightings of 1-2 Palmate newts from there between 1994 and 1999 but then no more reports until 3 newts, 1 a probable Smooth newt, were seen there in August 2004.

There was a sighting of a newt in a burn near Heldale water, Hoy on 16th July 1987.

# Amphibians

## TOADS : Bufonidae

Photo ©Keith Johnson

### COMMON TOAD *Bufo bufo*

Probably introduced, rare.

Found throughout Mainland Britain and 1 or 2 of the offshore islands

The skin is warty and usually brownish in colour with some darker blotches on the upperside, the underside is whitish. Males in the breeding season may have yellowish green on the underside. The largest female toad so far measured in Orkney was found in Birsay. It weighed 106gms and was 90.8mm in length. The males are smaller.

The first mention of toads in Orkney was by Wallace in 1693 who stated "there are some toads". Buckley and Harvie-Brown, in 1891, noted that the toad was common on all islands. There was a dramatic decline during the 20th century, particularly since about 1950. In the last 5 years there have only been records from Hoy and the north west of Mainland. Mainly nocturnal, toads are most active on mild damp nights and could be overlooked. Possible reasons for its decline are thought to be loss of habitat, with pollution and drainage of breeding pools. The spread of the hedgehog may be another factor as there are anecdotal reports of them eating toadlets as they emerge from the breeding pools.

Toads have been observed in their breeding habitat from 3rd April and small tadpoles seen on 9th May. During the day toads can be found under stones, hiding in holes in banks or low cliffs and under thick vegetation. On Hoy they have been found from just over sea level to above 200m on moorland. Latest sighting is 1st November.

## FROGS : Ranidae

### COMMON FROG *Rana temporaria*

Introduced, uncommon

Photo ©Chris Booth

Widespread throughout the British Isles, apart from some outlying islands; has been introduced into Shetland.

Compared to a toad, the frog has a rather pointed nose, the skin is smooth and shiny, variable in colour from grey brown to olive and yellow, with numerous black spots. Occasionally red or orange specimens are reported. Frogs up to 71gms in weight and 79.2mm in length have been recorded.

Frog bones have been found during excavation of archaeological sites and it seems possible that Neolithic settlers introduced frogs, perhaps as a source of food. Mention of frogs is made by both Wallace (1693) and Low at the end of the 18th century, but not by later writers, so it would appear that frogs must have become extinct at least early in the 19th century. During the 20th century there were numerous attempts to introduce frogs, particularly from the mid-1970's onwards, using spawn, tadpoles and adult animals. Frogs now seem to be well established in a number of islands with spawn being laid each year. Further introductions continue to take place.

Adult frogs have been reported as early as 14th January but the majority do not come out of hibernation until March. The earliest date for spawn is the 26th February but most is laid from mid-March to the end of the month. Froglets are seen from late June. The latest sighting of an adult frog is 15th November. Some tadpoles may overwinter. A live tadpole was found in mud at the bottom of a garden pond on 28th January.

Since 1980 there have been attempts to introduce both Slow worm *Anguis fragilis* (South Ronaldsay) and Common lizard *Lacerta vivipara* (East Mainland). These attempts do not appear to have been successful although slow worms did survive for several years.

## ORDER SQUAMATA

**Anguidae : Slow worm and Glass snake**

### SLOW WORM *Anguis fragilis* — **Introduced, probably extinct**

- 1 found on Stromness pier in 1964 was thought to have arrived amongst shipping cargo.
- Several were released in the early 1980's in South Ronaldsay and 1 was seen there in 1998. The last record from this site is of 1 found freshly dead on 5th April 1999.

### COMMON LIZARD *Lacerta vivipara* — **Introduced, probably extinct**

- Several common lizards were released in Toab, East Mainland in 1985, but there have been no further reports.

## MARINE TURTLES : Order Testudines

**SEA TURTLES : Dermochelidae and Chelonidae**

It is interesting that probably the first mention of turtles in British waters was given by Sibbald in 1684, who stated that a worthy man living in Orkney informed him that turtles were sometimes captured there. Wallace, in 1693, probably referring to turtles, noted that sometimes living tortoises were found on the shore. Buckley and Harvie-Brown recorded that Sibbald received the shell of a Hawksbill turtle *Eretmochelys imbricata* from Orkney.

Turtles must have been rare as the only other historical information found is that of an annotated note, written by Moodie-Heddle of Melsetter, in the margin of a copy of *Flora Scotica*, to the effect that 2 turtles had been caught in Orkney between 1840 and 1890.

Groundwater reported the sighting of a turtle, about 1m in length, off Halcro Head, South Ronaldsay in December 1964. Unfortunately it was not seen well enough to make a specific identification. He was also told of the stranding of a turtle on the east side of South Ronaldsay in the 1920's.

Since 1980, 3 species of turtle have been reported, the Leathery turtle, the Green turtle and the Loggerhead turtle, but only the former has been seen alive.

Sea turtles are found in tropical oceans around the world. Apart from the Leathery turtle they are rare visitors to northern Europe.

# Reptiles

## LEATHERY TURTLE *Dermochelys coriacea*

Rare

Photo ©Edwin Groat

The Leathery turtle has well developed thermoregulatory adaptations that allow it to survive in the colder waters of the north east Atlantic. These turtles move northwards in the summer following concentrations of jellyfish, which are their main prey. They then return south in the autumn.

The largest species of turtle, it can reach a length of up to 2.9m and a weight of 900kg. The carapace, or shell, is black in colour with lighter markings and 5-7 longitudinal ridges, some observers have described them as being like an upturned dinghy floating in the water.

There are no records of this species prior to 1987, since then there have been the following reports of live turtles :

- 1987 27th Aug 1 seen from a fishing boat off the east coast of Westray.
- 1993 15th Aug 1 seen from the MV Varagen between Start Point, Sanday and North Ronaldsay. It was moving south.
- 1993 Late Aug Probably the same turtle was seen from a fishing boat on two occasions off the Brough of Birsay.
- 1993 25th Oct 1 seen in Scapa Flow just south off Scapa Pier.
- 1997 19th Sep 1 off Bis Geos, Westray. It was entangled in creel ropes but was released and swam away, apparently unharmed.
- 2001 22nd Sep 1 entangled in creel ropes at the North Shoal, 12 miles north-west of the Brough of Birsay. It was successfully released. A turtle had been seen in this vicinity 2 days previously.

Since 1990 there have been 4 strandings of dead turtles between 23rd September and 12th November, while another turtle was found dead, entangled in creel ropes, in October 1996.

## GREEN TURTLE *Chelonia mydas*

Very rare

The shell in the adult is dark olive or grey with darker markings, the juvenile is chestnut coloured. Length up to 1.2m.

- 1 was found dead on the shore of the Loch of Stenness on 27th January 1980.

The length of the whole turtle was 40cm and the width was 28cm. Unfortunately nothing is known about the circumstances of its arrival on the shores of the loch.

## LOGGERHEAD TURTLE *Caretta caretta*

Very rare

Photo ©Chris Booth

The colour is reddish brown, juveniles have small spikes along spine of shell. Length up to 1.5m.

The only record is of a juvenile found dead amongst seaweed on the shore of the Choin, Marwick, Birsay on 23rd July 2002. The total length was 38cm and the carapace was 29cm long and 27cm wide.

Turtle sp.

A large turtle was seen off  Seal Skerry, North Ronaldsay on 4th October 1999.  It was thought to be a Leathery turtle but it was not possible to get a close view to confirm the identification.

Gannets, Noup Head, Westray. Chris Booth

# Birds

Orkney is an important area for birds. In spring and autumn large numbers pass through the islands on migration and among them are usually several national rarities to delight birdwatchers.

Sheltered areas on the east side of the islands are often the best places to look for migrants and the island of North Ronaldsay, in particular, is well worth a visit. Sandy beaches can attract waders, such as those of Deerness and Scapa on Mainland, and the island of Sanday.

In the summer months the cliffs hold large colonies of breeding seabirds. These can be found, for example, in West Mainland at Row Head, Marwick Head and the Brough of Birsay, and to the east at Mull Head and the island of Copinsay. In the North Isles, Westray has spectacular colonies at Noup Head and Puffins are easily seen at the Castle o' Burrien. The North Hill on Papa Westray usually has many breeding terns as well as Arctic skuas. Unfortunately the breeding season of 2004 was disastrous for Orkney's seabirds and it remains to be seen if the large numbers that are usually present will return in future years.

Waders breed in the wetlands throughout the islands. The moorlands of Hoy, Mainland and Rousay may hold several raptor species, together with waders, Arctic and Great skuas. Red-throated divers also breed here, as well as on the Mill Loch in Eday.

During the winter, wildfowl can be found on the fresh water lochs, as well as on sheltered sea areas. Scapa Flow and the Lochs of Harray and Stenness hold some of the largest numbers, while in low lying fields and around the shoreline, flocks of feeding waders can be seen.

# Birds

This systematic list of birds follows the taxonomic recommendations for British birds given by Knox A G, Collinson M, Helbig A J, Parkin D P, Sangster G. 2002. *Ibis* 144:707-710. Only records of rarities that have been accepted by the relevant rarities committees have been included. The list covers most records up to the end of 2004 but there are some rarities still under consideration.

English names are those that are at present in common usage.

The birds of Orkney have been well documented in recent years so that assessments of their status are probably more accurate than for other vertebrate groups. In an attempt to standardise the description of the status of each species, the following nomenclature has been used:

| | | |
|---|---|---|
| Very rare | Up to 10 breeding records in total | Up to 10 records in total |
| | **Annual number of breeding pairs** | **Annual number of non-breeding individuals** |
| Rare | 1-10 | 1-10 |
| Uncommon | 11-100 | 11-100 |
| Fairly common | 101-1,000 | 101-1,000 |
| Common | 1,001-10,000 | 1,001-10,000 |
| Abundant | 10,000+ | 10,000+ |

# BIRDWATCHING

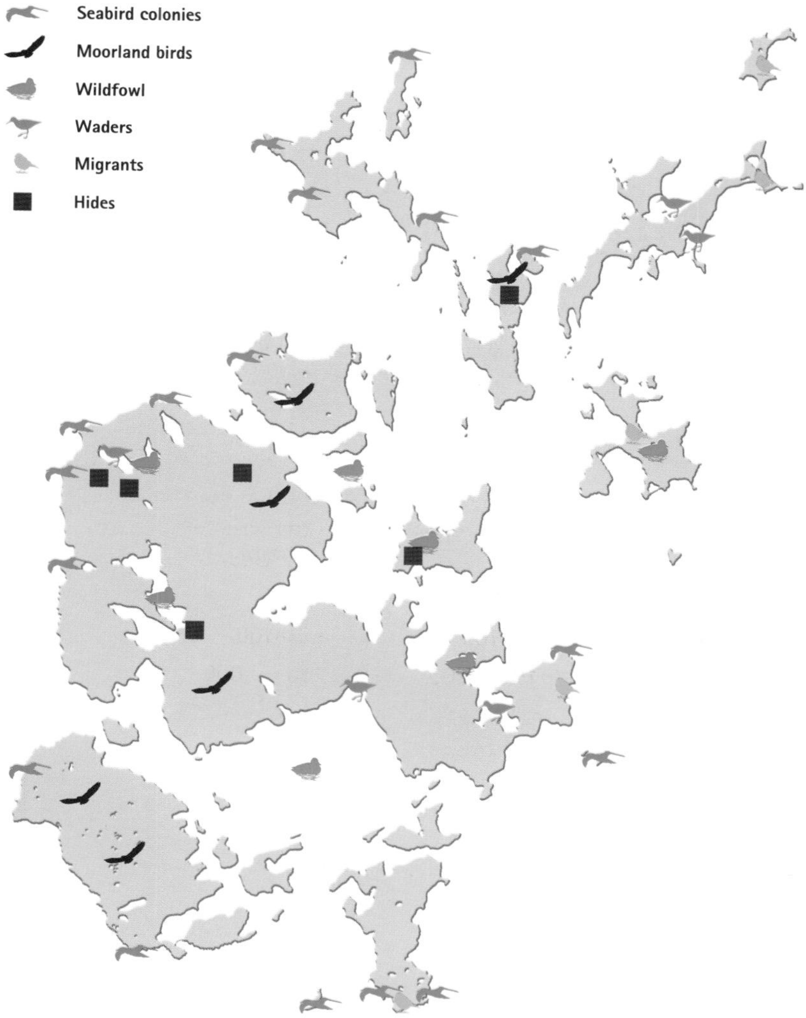

# Birds

## SWANS, GEESE AND DUCKS : Anatidae

Photo ©Ian Hourston

### MUTE SWAN *Cygnus olor*

Well distributed as a breeding species, especially in the larger islands, apart from Hoy

The breeding population has fluctuated, especially on the Loch of Harray. A complete census of the county in 2002 found 128 breeding pairs and 50 territorial pairs. In addition 312 non-breeding birds were counted.

### BEWICK'S SWAN *Cygnus columbianus*

Rare visitor

In the period 1973-2004 there have been only 9 records. These have involved 1-3 birds (January to April and October to December) .

### WHOOPER SWAN *Cygnus cygnus*

Fairly common passage and winter visitor with a few, mainly injured birds, summering

Photo ©Chris Booth

Birds start arriving in late September and the majority have left by the following April. 284 were counted in January 1995, during a survey of the islands.

### BEAN GOOSE *Anser fabalis*

Rare winter visitor, occasionally uncommon

Mainly 1-2 birds, with a maximum of 8, recorded from October to April. Single records for May and June.

Sightings have involved both **Taiga Bean Goose** *A.f.fabalis* and **Tundra Bean Goose** *A.f.rossicus*, the former race being the most frequent.

### PINK-FOOTED GOOSE *Anser brachyrhynchus*

Usually a fairly common passage visitor but occasionally common; small but increasing numbers present in winter

First migrants usually arrive in mid-September with last spring birds seen in May or early June.

## WHITE-FRONTED GOOSE *Anser albifrons*

**Greenland race** : *Anser a. flavirostris*

Fairly common but localised winter visitor and passage migrant

Flocks of over 100 may winter in the West Mainland, with smaller numbers at other sites. First birds arrive in September and the majority have left by end of April.

**European race** : *Anser a. albifrons*

Usually a rare winter visitor

Majority of reports are of 1-6 birds but in 1995 up to 42 were present in 1 flock from December to March 1996.

Photo ©Rod Thorne

## GREYLAG GOOSE *Anser anser*

Fairly common breeding species, common passage and winter visitor

Present throughout the year. Numbers of breeding pairs appear to increase annually. Over 43,000 birds may be in the islands at any one time during autumn and winter.

## SNOW GOOSE *Anser caerulescens*

Rare visitor

Between 1967 and 2004, there were 13 records from March to July involving 1-8 birds, and 5 records of between 1 and 6 birds from September to November.

## CANADA GOOSE *Branta canadensis*

In most years a rare visitor but occasionally uncommon

Recorded throughout the year, but with a majority of records from April to July. Maximum flock recorded is 23.

## BARNACLE GOOSE *Branta leucopsis*

A common, but localised, winter visitor having increased during the last 20 years. Also a passage visitor with occasional birds, probably injured, present in summer

The wintering flock in South Walls has now reached over 1,500 birds. Usually the first birds arrive in late September and most have left by early May.

Colour ringed birds from both the Greenland and Spitzbergen populations have been reported.

## BRENT GOOSE (Horra goose) *Branta bernicla*

An uncommon visitor but in some years may be rare

Although recorded in all months, with occasional birds wintering, main passage noted April and May; September and October. Birds of both **Dark-bellied race** *Branta b. bernicla* and **Light-bellied race** *Branta b. hrota* have been recorded, the latter being slightly commoner.

## RUDDY SHELDUCK *Tadorna ferruginea*

Very rare

5 records : June 1909, May 1932, May 1966 (pair), August 1990 and August to September 2000.

## SHELDUCK (Sly goose) *Tadorna tadorna*

Fairly common breeding species; rare September to November

Birds begin to return in late October, with a build up of numbers continuing into May. The majority of breeding birds have left the islands by the end of August. From a survey in 1992 it was estimated that there was a total of 105 territorial pairs distributed throughout the islands.

**MANDARIN DUCK** *Aix galericulata* Very rare

8 records. Apart from a pair in May 1979, all other sightings are of single birds, 6 of which were definitely males; 5 records between 8th April and 10th June, and 2 between 7th September and 28th October.

**WIGEON** *Anas penelope* Uncommon to fairly common breeding species; common on passage and in winter when present in both salt and fresh water

In winter largest numbers are found on the Loch of Harray, where monthly counts of over 5,000 have been recorded; elsewhere counts of over 1,000 are not uncommon.

**AMERICAN WIGEON** *Anas americana* Rare

There are 23 records between 1980 and 2004. Reported in all months except July and August, some birds were present in the same area for several months. Pairs have been recorded on 2 occasions, all other sightings are of single males.

**GADWALL** *Anas strepera* Rare breeding species; uncommon passage migrant

Confirmed breeding has been recorded from a number of localities including : Mainland - Birsay Moors, Holm, Loch of Banks, Loch of Tankerness, The Loons Birsay (up to 6 pairs); North Ronaldsay (up to 7 pairs); Papa Westray; Sanday; Shapinsay - Milldam (up to 4 pairs). Highest numbers recorded from September to April, maximum monthly count 45 on North Ronaldsay March 2002.

**TEAL** *Anas crecca* Fairly common breeding species, common on passage and in winter

Breeding pairs are found throughout the islands. In winter highest numbers have been reported from Shapinsay, with a peak count of 2,650 on 13th October 2002. Elsewhere counts of up to 300 are not uncommon.

**GREEN-WINGED TEAL** *Anas carolinensis* Rare

There are 13 records of this American duck between 1973 and 2004 : April and May - 4, October to March - 9.

**MALLARD (Stock duck)** *Anas platyrhynchos* Common breeding species, passage and winter visitor

Widespread throughout the islands.

Photo Stuart Williams

**PINTAIL** *Anas acuta* Uncommon breeding summer visitor, uncommon in winter and on passage

A survey in 1994 found that between 24 and 30 pairs may have attempted to breed. The highest autumn count is 95 on North Ronaldsay on 26th September 2004.

**GARGANEY** *Anas querquedula* Very rare breeding species. Usually a rare visitor, but occasionally uncommon

The only confirmed breeding record is on Papa Westray in 1999. Breeding has been suspected at other sites on several occasions over the years but never proved. Most records are from March to June, but has also been recorded from July to September.

# Birds

**BLUE-WINGED TEAL** *Anas discors* Very rare visitor

There are 9 records of this American species, 4 in spring between 2nd May and 23rd June, 5 in autumn between 5th September and 10th November.

**SHOVELER** *Anas clypeata* Uncommon summer visitor, resident in the North Isles

Breeds in small numbers in suitable localities throughout the islands. Maximum autumn count is 234 on Shapinsay on 17th October 1999.

**RED-CRESTED POCHARD** *Netta rufina* Very rare visitor

Between 5 and 8 individuals recorded since 1984. Sightings were all within the period 15th October to 14th March and some may refer to the same bird.

**COMMON POCHARD** *Aythya ferina* Common winter visitor, rare breeding species

Since 1996 breeding has been recorded in most years with 1-4 pairs on North Ronaldsay and on Shapinsay. Highest numbers are reported from October to March and over 1,000 birds may be present mid-winter.

**RING-NECKED DUCK** *Aythya collaris* Very rare

Only 2 records, both of single birds : 13th May to 16th June 1984 in Holm and in Orphir; 11th to 13th October 1988 at Loch of Harray.

**FERRUGINOUS DUCK** *Aythya nyroca* Very rare

The only record is of a male in Birsay on 24th May 1981.

**TUFTED DUCK** *Aythia fuligula* Fairly common breeding species, common in winter

Widespread as a breeding species. Wintering numbers build up in September, declining again in March.

**SCAUP** *Aythya marila* Very rare breeding species, fairly common but localised winter visitor

Breeding records 1954-1959, 1965, 1969, 1973, 1978 and 1979. Main wintering flock is found on either the Lochs of Harray or Stenness, with counts of over 400. Elsewhere only 1-15 birds are recorded.

**LESSER SCAUP** *Aythya affinis* Very rare visitor

There are 2 records, both of single females : Loch of Tankerness from 7th December 1998 to 10th January 1999; Loch of Harray from 22nd February to 30th March 2000.

Photo: Chris Booth

**EIDER (Dunter)** *Somateria mollissima* Common resident and probable winter visitor

Widespread as a breeding species, particularly on uninhabited islands and holms. In November 1998 a total of 2,308 counted in Scapa Flow.

**KING EIDER** *Somateria spectabilis* Rare visitor

Between 1975 and 2004 there have been 8 records, 3 between October and February, and 5 in May and June.

**STELLER'S EIDER** *Polysticta stelleri* Very rare visitor

There are 9 records, 5 of which probably refer to the same male bird which was recorded annually from late April to late August in the Papa Westray/Westray area between 1975 and 1982. The other records have been in the following months : January - 1, April - 1, October/November - 2.

**LONG-TAILED DUCK (Caloo)** *Clangula hyemalis* Common winter visitor; has bred

Photo ©P & V Reynolds

Recorded throughout the year but usually only 1 or 2 birds are present in mid-summer. There is a breeding record for 1911 and pairs probably bred in 1912 and 1926. In autumn the first returning birds arrive in late September and early October and in the spring the majority have left by the end of May. 1,582 were counted in Scapa Flow in January 1999.

**COMMON SCOTER** *Melanitta nigra* Uncommon visitor; has bred

Recorded in all months. There is some indication of passage, with an increase in numbers during April and May; September and October. Maximum flock count is 50. Breeding was recorded on a number of occasions between 1927 and 1955.

**SURF SCOTER** *Melanitta perspicillata* Rare visitor

Rather irregular with records in all months. Most frequently reported from April to June and September to December, usually single birds.

**VELVET SCOTER (Velvet duck)** *Melanitta fusca* Fairly common winter visitor

Recorded regularly from January to May and then from September to December, with occasional sightings in the summer months.

**GOLDENEYE** *Bucephala clangula* Fairly common winter visitor with occasional birds recorded in summer months

Found on both fresh and salt water. The largest numbers are reported from Lochs of Harray and Stenness and from Scapa Flow.

**SMEW** *Mergellus albellus* Rare winter visitor

Since 1980, 1-4 birds are recorded annually from October to May.

**RED-BREASTED MERGANSER** *Mergus serrator* **(Sawbill, Harle)** Fairly common breeding species and winter visitor

Breeding pairs are well distributed throughout the islands. Largest flock counts are usually recorded during April and May and August to November.

**GOOSANDER** *Mergus merganser* — A rare visitor but recorded regularly

Sightings in all months, but most frequent from October to April.

**RUDDY DUCK** *Oxyura jamaicensis* — Uncommon visitor; rare breeding species

The only breeding records are from Graemeshall Loch, Holm and more regularly Mill Dam, Shapinsay. Elsewhere it is most often recorded from April to June and October to November, with occasional sightings at other times.

## GROUSE : Tetraonidae

Photo ©P & V Reynolds

**RED GROUSE** *Lagopus lagopus* — Fairly common resident breeding species

Confined to moorland areas, does not breed on the islands north of Rousay and Stronsay.

**PTARMIGAN** *Lagopus muta*

Extinct about 1831, formerly bred and was confined to Hoy.

**BLACK GROUSE** *Tetrao tetrix* — **Introduction in 19th century failed; extinct**

The origin of the birds recorded in 1958 and 1962 must be considered doubtful because of possible further introduction attempts.

## PARTRIDGES and PHEASANTS : Phasianidae

**RED-LEGGED PARTRIDGE** *Alectoris rufa* — Introduced

An attempted introduction in 1840 failed. More recently 2 were seen on Shapinsay in October 2001 and single birds on Shapinsay and in Holm in 2002. A pair with 4 young was reported from Shapinsay in 2003. Further introductions were made in 2004.

**GREY PARTRIDGE** *Perdix perdix* — Introduced

There have been several attempted introductions. On Shapinsay some of the birds bred in the wild and a brood of young was seen in 1993. 3 were seen near the Loch of Tankerness on 19th August 1998.

**QUAIL** *Coturnix coturnix* — Usually a rare, but sometimes an uncommon summer visitor; occasionally breeds

The only definite breeding records in recent years were in 1982, 1992 and 1993, but calling birds have been heard during summer each year since 1987. Extreme dates 20th April and 30th October.

**PHEASANT** *Phasianus colchicus* — Fairly common introduced species

Now breeding and well established on several islands. Further introductions are still taking place.

## DIVERS : Gaviidae

**RED-THROATED DIVER (Rain goose)** *Gavia stellata* — Fairly common breeding species, uncommon in January and December

Photo ©Stuart Williams

Approximately 130 pairs breed annually, with highest numbers on Hoy, but breeding pairs are also present on Eday, Fara, Mainland, Rousay, Shapinsay and Stronsay.

The Mill Loch, Eday holds the largest concentration of breeding pairs.

Counts of up to 22 birds are recorded in mid-winter.

**BLACK-THROATED DIVER** *Gavia arctica* Uncommon passage and winter visitor

Recorded in all months, with highest numbers from October through to early May. The maximum monthly count for Scapa Flow is 57 in December 1998. The largest single gathering noted has been 40 off Hobbister, Orphir on 7th May 2002.

**GREAT NORTHERN DIVER (Immer goose)** *Gavia immer* Fairly common to common winter visitor, uncommon in mid-summer

Gatherings of up to 80 birds are not uncommon in favoured localities such as Scapa Flow and Deer Sound/Shapinsay Sound from October to May. Increase in numbers during late April/early May, but then usually only 1-4, mainly immature birds, are recorded from June to September.

The maximum monthly count for Scapa Flow is 781 in March 1999.

**WHITE-BILLED DIVER** *Gavia adamsii* Rare visitor

Over 20 records, all since 1976. Apart from 1 on 1st July, all records have been within the period 1st October to 7th June. There is a slight peak of sightings in April and May.

## GREBES : Podicepedidae

**LITTLE GREBE (Dabchick, Little footyarse)** *Tachybaptus ruficollis* Rare breeding species, uncommon in winter

Since 1990 breeding of 1-2 pairs has been confirmed at sites on the following islands : Burray (1), Mainland (2), Rousay (1), Shapinsay (1) and Westray (2). It has also been suspected at a number of other sites. The maximum number of pairs proved to breed in any 1 year has been 6. Widely distributed in winter in small numbers of mainly 1-5 birds and a maximum count of 10 at any 1 locality.

**GREAT CRESTED GREBE** *Podiceps cristatus* Rare visitor

There are records in the periods January to June and September to December. Apart from 1 sighting of 3, all other reports are of single birds.

**RED-NECKED GREBE** *Podiceps grisegena* Rare visitor

1-6 birds are regularly recorded from January to May and September to December on both salt and fresh water, with occasional records from June to August. 23 were present in Scapa Flow in March 1999.

**SLAVONIAN GREBE** *Podiceps auritus* Uncommon winter and passage visitor

Regularly recorded from sheltered areas of salt water and some fresh water lochs from January to May and September to December, rare at other times. The maximum monthly count for Scapa Flow is 124 in January 1999.

**BLACK-NECKED GREBE** *Podiceps nigricollis* Very rare visitor

There is a record of 1 in 1873 and more recently of single birds on North Ronaldsay on 1st and 4th June 1989, at Bay of Sandoyne, Holm on 15th April 1997 and Loch of Tankerness 17th-25th April, 2004.

## ALBATROSSES : Diomedeidae

**BLACK-BROWED ALBATROSS** *Thalassarche melanophri* Very rare

Photo ©Chris Booth

2 records : 1 off Hoy on 13th August 1969 and the other in Scapa Flow on 21st August 1975.

An Albatross, not specifically identified, was seen in the Pentland Firth on 4th Sept. 1995.

## PETRELS and SHEARWATERS : Procellariidae

Photo ©lChris Booth

### FULMAR (Mallimack) *Fulmarus glacialis*

Abundant resident breeding species

Nests not only on sea cliffs, but also at a variety of inland sites. 90,846 apparently occupied nest sites were located in the Seabird 2000 census.

### FEA'S/ZINO'S PETREL *Pterodroma feae/madeira*

Very rare

The only record is of 1 seen off North Ronaldsay on 22nd September 2002.

### CORY'S SHEARWATER *Calonectris diomedea*

Rare visitor

There have been 12 records, all since 1970 and between 27th June and 17th October, but most frequent in September. Apart from 1 record of 5, all the rest were of single birds.

### GREAT SHEARWATER *Puffinus gravis*

Rare visitor

There are 12 records. 1 of 2 birds and the rest of single birds and in the following months : August - 2, September - 6, October - 4

### SOOTY SHEARWATER *Puffinus griseus*

Common autumn passage visitor

Regularly recorded from July to October, sometimes in quite large numbers, especially in late August and during September. Occasional records March to June, November and December.

### MANX SHEARWATER *Puffinus puffinus* (Lyre, Lyrie)

Uncommon but decreasing breeding species, fairly common passage migrant

Breeding colonies, which are only small in size, now confined to Hoy. Recorded on passage from April to November, but majority of reports are in August and September. Very rare at other times.

### BALEARIC SHEARWATER *Puffinus mauretanicus*

Rare visitor

Accepted as Balearic Shearwater *Puffinus mauretanicus*, 1981-1991, 2003 : 6 records, 1 in August and 5 in September.

Accepted as *Puffinus yelkouan*, 1993-1997 : 7 records, June to November.

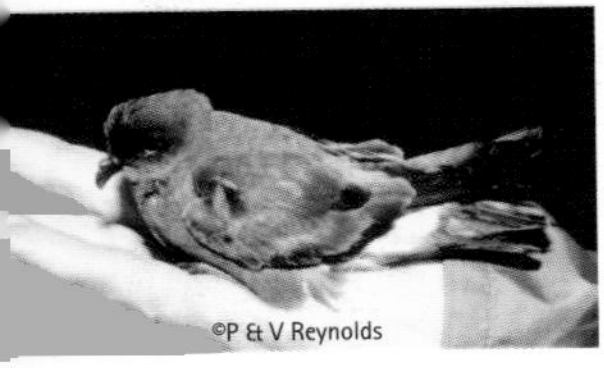
©P & V Reynolds

### STORM PETREL (Storm finch) *Hydrobates pelagicus*

Common breeding summer visitor

There are colonies on a number of the remoter islands. The Seabird 2000 census found 1,870 apparently occupied sites, the largest colonies being on Auskerry and Sule Skerry. Noted offshore from March to November.

## LEACH'S STORM-PETREL *Oceanodroma leucorhoa*

Possibly rare breeding species and uncommon summer visitor

Said to have bred on Sule Skerry in 1934 and birds have been noted there on visits from 1975 onwards. Recorded regularly offshore from late May to early November.

### GANNETS : Sulidae

## GANNET (Solan goose) *Morus bassanus*

Common breeding species and passage visitor

There is a large colony on Sule Stack, where a survey in 1994 found 4,888 apparently occupied sites. In 2003 15 nests were found on Sule Skerry and 5 pairs attempted to nest on the Noup cliffs, Westray, where 1 young was reared. There were 14 pairs on the Noup cliffs, Westray in 2004. Occasionally seen ashore at other sites, particularly the Horse of Copinsay. Present offshore throughout the year.

Photo ©Chris Booth

### CORMORANTS : Phalacrocoracidae

## CORMORANT (Great scarf, Hibling) *Phalacrocorax carbo*

Fairly common resident breeding species

Has declined in recent years; 412 nests in 7 colonies were found in the Seabird 2000 census, compared to 570 nests in 8 colonies in 1985 and over 600 nests in the late 1960's.

## SHAG (Scarf or Tappie whaesie) *Phalacrocorax aristotelis*

Common, but probably declining, resident breeding species

The Seabird 2000 census found 1,872 apparently occupied nests. Gatherings of up to 400 birds are not uncommon outside the breeding season.

Photo ©Drew Kennedy

Photo ©Ian Hourston

## HERONS and BITTERNS : Ardeidae

### BITTERN *Botaurus stellaris*
Very rare

There are 5 records, all of single birds : Voy, Sandwick on 22nd February 1934; The Loons, Birsay on 29th October 1996; Backaskaill Loch, Papa Westray on 3rd-5th May 2000; Skaill, Eday on 5th January 2001 and probably the same bird Evie, Mainland on 7th January; North Ronaldsay 5th March 2003.

### LITTLE BITTERN *Ixobrychus minutus*
Very rare

There are 3 records, all of single birds : On Sanday in 1806; Loch of Stenness on 14th May 1909 and North Ronaldsay on 31st May 1971.

### NIGHT HERON *Nycticorax nycticorax*
Very rare

6 records, all of single birds : 1st November 1961, 23rd-24th May 1982, 23rd-25th May 1986, 6th July 1989, 23rd-29th March 1993,19th-20th May 1998.

### SQUACCO HERON *Ardeola ralloides*
Very rare

The only record is of 1 shot on North Ronaldsay on 7th September 1896.

### LITTLE EGRET *Egretta garzetta*
Very rare

There are 10 records, all of single birds, extreme dates are 15th May and 13th December, some staying for several weeks.

### GREAT WHITE EGRET *Ardea alba*
Very rare

There are 2 records, both of single birds and on North Ronaldsay : 28th and 29th April 1978; 2nd May 2002.

### GREY HERON *Ardea cinerea*
Formerly a rare breeding species, now probably very rare; fairly common passage and winter visitor

Between 1990 and 1998, 7-11 pairs bred annually in 1 colony. In 1999 there were only 6 pairs, falling to 2 in 2001 and 1 in 2003 and none in 2004. Occasionally single pairs are reported breeding at other localities. First passage and wintering birds arrive in July and the majority have left by end of April.

### PURPLE HERON *Ardea purpurea*
Very rare

Only 2 records : 1st-8th September 1980 on North Ronaldsay and 2nd-5th August 1982 on South Ronaldsay.

## STORKS : Ciconiidae

### BLACK STORK *Ciconia nigra*
Very rare

Recorded on 3 occasions : 7th-12th June 1972 in Sandwick, Mainland; 23rd and 24th June 1990 on Sanday and 27th June 1995 on Hoy.

### WHITE STORK *Ciconia ciconia*
Very rare

6 records : In 1840; May 1971, June 1972, April-June 1977, April 1983 and April 2002.

## IBISES and SPOONBILLS : Threskiornithidae

### GLOSSY IBIS *Plegadis falcinellus*
Very rare

5 records : September 1857 (1), September 1903 (1), September to October 1907 (19 or 20), September 1986-January 1987 (1), 5th January 2000 (1).

## SPOONBILL *Platalea leucorodia*

Very rare

There were 5 records in 19th century involving 1-9 birds. 20th century records, of single birds, are October 1939, June 1975 and May 1996. 2 were seen in October 1998.

### KITES, VULTURES, HARRIERS, HAWKS, BUZZARDS, EAGLES : Accipitridae

## HONEY BUZZARD *Pernis apivorus*

A rare but regular visitor

Extreme dates for sightings are 30th April and 4th October. Highest annual total is 6 records, but more often only 1-2 reported in a year.

## BLACK KITE *Milvus migrans*

Very rare visitor

There are 7 records between 1966 and 2004, all of single birds : May 5, June 1, September 1.

## RED KITE *Milvus milvus*

Very rare visitor

There were 2 records in the 19th century, in 1877 and 1878. In April 1988 there were 6 reports of a single bird from various locations, which may all have referred to the same individual. Sightings of single birds in 1989, 1992, 1993, 1994, 2002 and 2 in 2003. Some had wing tags and were probably from the re-introduction scheme in the Highlands.

## WHITE-TAILED EAGLE (Erne) *Halaietus albicilla*

Rare visitor, formerly bred

The last definite breeding attempt was in 1873, but may possibly have bred in 1877 and 1911. Between 1976 and 2004 there have been sightings of single birds in 16 of these years, involving a minimum of 26 individuals. At least 3 of these have been wing-tagged and were from the Scottish re-introduction programme.

## MARSH HARRIER *Circus aeruginosus*

Very rare breeding species and rare/uncommon visitor.

2 pairs bred successfully in 2001 and 1 pair in 2003 and 2004. Extreme dates are 16th February and 20th November, but most often reported in May.

## HEN HARRIER (Gos-haak) *Circus cyaneus*

Uncommon resident breeding species; passage migrant and winter visitor

Photos ©P & V Reynolds

Numbers of breeding females declined from over 90 in 1978 to a low of 28 in 1996 but have since increased and there were 67 occupied sites in 2004. Breeding birds in 2004 reported from Hoy, Mainland and Rousay.

## PALLID HARRIER *Circus macrourus*

Very rare

There is 1 record, that of a male which was present in the West Mainland from April to at least September 1995. It paired with a female Hen Harrier, but the breeding attempt failed.

**MONTAGU'S HARRIER** *Circus pygargus* — Very rare

The only authenticated record is of a male on North Ronaldsay on 20th May 1996.

**GOSHAWK** *Accipiter gentilis* — Rare visitor

Between 1968 and 2004 there have been 18 records in the period February to June and 5 from September to December. All have been of single birds.

**SPARROWHAWK** *Accipiter nisus* — Rare breeding resident; uncommon on passage

Breeding population probably between 6 and 10 pairs annually. Main passage movements are noted March to May and September to November.

**COMMON BUZZARD** *Buteo buteo* — Rare resident breeding species; uncommon passage visitor

During the last 10 years between 1 and 3 pairs have bred annually. Away from breeding areas the majority of sightings have been recorded from January to May and August to December.

**ROUGH-LEGGED BUZZARD** *Buteo lagopus* — Rare passage and winter visitor

1-2 birds are recorded most years, with the majority of records from March to May and October to December. Occasionally a bird may overwinter.

**GOLDEN EAGLE** *Aquila chrysaetos* — Rare visitor; formerly bred

A single pair bred regularly between 1966 and 1982, since then 1-2 birds were recorded annually from 1983 up until 1992. There were no more records until single birds were seen in April 2001, March 2002 and March 2003.

## OSPREYS : Pandionidae

**OSPREY** *Pandion haliaetus* — Rare visitor

There are between 1 and 8 records annually with the majority of sightings in May and June, less frequent from August to October. Extreme dates 4th April and 27th October.

## FALCONS : Falconidae

**KESTREL** *Falco tinnunculus* — An uncommon resident breeding species but decreasing; uncommon passage and winter visitor
**(Moosie haak, Wind cuffer)**

Photo ©P & V Reynolds

Has declined as a breeding species in the last 25 years. Probably now only about 20-25 pairs attempt to breed in any 1 year.

**RED-FOOTED FALCON** *Falco vespertinus* Rare visitor

There are 15 records from 1962-2004, 14 of single birds and 1 of 2 birds. In spring 13 records between 8th May and 18th June, in autumn 2 records between 11th August and 10th September.

**MERLIN** *Falco columbarius* Uncommon breeding species; passage and winter visitor

14-21 sites have been thought to be occupied annually during the last 5 years.

Main passage movements from March to April and September to November.

**HOBBY** *Falco subbuteo* Rare visitor

Since 1986 there have been 1-6 records annually, all involving single birds. Extreme dates 24th April and 23rd September.

**GYR FALCON** *Falco rusticolus* Rare visitor

Over 20 records, including those from the 19th and early 20th centuries. The majority of sightings since 1984 have been in the period January to June with only 2 in November and December.

**PEREGRINE** *Falco peregrinus* Uncommon resident breeding species, probably declining

Between 11 and 19 pairs are thought to have attempted to breed annually since 1991.

## RAILS, CRAKES and COOTS : Rallidae

**WATER RAIL** *Rallus aquaticus* Rare breeding species; uncommon passage and winter visitor

Recorded throughout the year. It appears to be increasing as a breeding species with confirmed reports from : Mainland - Graemeshall Loch Holm, The Loons and St.Ola; North Ronaldsay; Papa Westray and Shapinsay.

**SPOTTED CRAKE** *Porzana porzana* Very rare breeding species and rare visitor

A pair were presumed to have bred on Egilsay in 2000. Since 1968 most often reported from North Ronaldsay and Egilsay with the majority of records in May, September and October. Extreme dates 22nd April and 24th November.

**CORNCRAKE** *Crex crex* Uncommon breeding summer and passage visitor which declined in 20th century

This species was much commoner in the early part of 20th century. A survey in 1979 found 102-104 calling males but in 1993 only 6 calling males were reported. In recent years numbers of calling males have fluctuated, with 11 in 2000, 9 in 2001, 16 in 2002, 31 in 2003 but only 16 in 2004. Since 1973 the earliest calling date is 16th April and the last reported sighting on 23rd October.

**MOORHEN** **(Water hen)** *Gallinula chloropus* Fairly common breeding species; passage and winter visitor

May have declined as a breeding species in some areas due to loss of breeding habitat. Maximum numbers are recorded from September to February. Highest recorded count is 92 at Bu Farm, Burray on 31st December 1999.

**COOT** **(Snaith, Snysen)** *Fulica atra* — Uncommon breeding species; fairly common winter visitor

Widespread in small numbers as a breeding species throughout the larger islands, apart from Hoy. There is a large wintering flock on Loch of Harray with numbers building up from late September and declining in March. Maximum count recorded there is 972 in November 1995.

## CRANES : Gruidae

Photo ©Stuart Williams

**CRANE** *Grus grus* — Rare visitor

Recorded most years with the majority of sightings in May, occasionally birds stay for several weeks. Extreme dates are 28th March and 4th November. Sightings have involved 1-4 birds.

## BUSTARDS : Otididae

**LITTLE BUSTARD** *Tetrax tetrax* — Very rare

There is only 1 record, a male on North Ronaldsay on 23rd May 1989.

**GREAT BUSTARD** *Otis tarda* — Very rare

There are 3 records of single birds, all of which were females. 2 were from Stronsay on 29th March 1876 and 8th February 1892, the other from Sanday on 4th January 1924.

## OYSTERCATCHERS : Haematopodidae

Photo ©Chris Booth

**OYSTERCATCHER** *Haematopus ostralegus*
**(Skeldro, Chaldro)** — Common breeding species, also a passage visitor; less numerous in winter and on passage

Returning birds are usually noted from mid-February, with numbers declining in October. Winter coastline population is estimated at 2,700 birds. Has increased as a breeding species during the 20th century and spread into inland habitats, with a breeding population of over 9,000 pairs.

## STILTS and AVOCETS : Recurvirostridae

**BLACK-WINGED STILT** *Himantopus himantopus* — Very rare

The only record is of 2 killed at Lopness, Sanday in 1814.

**AVOCET** *Recurvirostra avosetta* — Very rare

Since 1934 there have been 6 records, 1 of 2 birds and 5 of single birds. Extreme dates 30th March and 6th July.

## STONE CURLEWS (THICK-KNEES) and STONE PLOVERS : Burhinidae

**STONE CURLEW** *Burhinus oedicnemus* — Very rare

The only record is of 1 in Holm from 29th June to 2nd July 1990.

## COURSERS and PRATINCOLES : Glareolidae

**COLLARED PRATINCOLE** *Glareola pratincola* — Very rare

There are 2 records, 1 on South Ronaldsay on 6th October 1963 and 1 at the Loch of Tankerness on 30th May 2003.

## PLOVERS : Charadriidae

### LITTLE RINGED PLOVER *Charadrius dubius*
Very rare

5 records, all of single birds : Stronsay 27th September to 2nd October 1993, North Ronaldsay 10th and 11th May 1994, Deerness 25th May 1994, Loch of Tankerness 3rd May 2002 and 5th May 2004.

### RINGED PLOVER *Charadrius hiaticula*
**(Sand lark, Sinloo)**
Fairly common breeding species; common on passage and in winter

A survey in 1984 found 535 pairs on territory at both coastal and inland sites. Winter coastline population is estimated at 1,600 birds.

### GREATER SAND PLOVER *Charadrius leschenaultii*
Very rare

There is 1 record, that of a bird present in Deerness from 9th-16th June 1979.

### DOTTEREL *Charadrius morinellus*
Mainly a rare visitor but occasionally uncommon; has bred

The only breeding record was in 1850. Since 1987 it has been recorded annually, except for 2002. Most frequently recorded in spring, with majority in May, extreme dates 13th April and 28th June. Maximum flock size recorded is 14. Autumn : 1-6 birds, extreme dates 7th August and 5th October.

### AMERICAN GOLDEN PLOVER *Pluvialis dominica*
Very rare

There are 14 records with extreme dates 24th August and 6th December. All are of single birds apart from 2 seen feeding in the same field in September 1996.

### PACIFIC GOLDEN PLOVER *Pluvialis fulva*
Very rare

There are 6 records, all of single birds, with extreme dates 8th July and 26th November.

### GOLDEN PLOVER **(Pliver)** *Pluvialis apricaria*
Uncommon breeding species, common in winter and on passage

Has declined as a breeding species, particularly in the latter half of the 20th century. The main breeding grounds are on the moorlands of Hoy, Mainland and Rousay. Spring passage noticeable in April and May and first returning wintering birds arrive at end of June; large flocks of up to 2,000 birds are not unusual in October and November. Wintering population estimated at 4,000 but numbers decline quickly in bad weather.

### GREY PLOVER *Pluvialis squatarola*
Uncommon passage and winter visitor

Small numbers have been reported throughout the year but not recorded regularly in June and July. Most numerous and widespread on passage in April and May and then September and October. Highest counts have been reported from Sanday, with a maximum from there of 105 East Sanday in February 1994.

### SOCIABLE PLOVER *Vanellus gregarius*
Very rare

There are only 3 records, all of single birds : 3rd November 1926 on North Ronaldsay; December 1949 in Rendall and 15th January 1969 on Eday.

### LAPWING **(Teeick, Teeo)** *Vanellus vanellus*
Common breeding species; common in winter and on passage

Common and well distributed as a breeding species. Numbers are lower now than in the early

part of the 20th century, probably due to loss of habitat through land drainage, breeding population is now about 5,000 pairs. Post breeding flocks start building up at end of June. During the autumn and winter flocks of up to 500 birds are not uncommon. Many birds leave the islands during snow cover.

## SANDPIPERS, STINTS, GODWITS, CURLEWS, SNIPES, PHALAROPES : Scolopacidae

### KNOT *Calidris canutus*

Fairly common passage and winter visitor

In spring, main passage occurs in late April and in May. A maximum flock count of 1,250 was recorded at Holm on 6th May 1984, but such large flocks are unusual. Autumn movements are most noticeable from late July to end of October, often involving over 100 birds. Smaller numbers present in suitable localities during winter but there were 361 at Mill Sands, Tankerness on 22nd February 2001.

### SANDERLING *Calidris alba*

Fairly common but localised passage and winter visitor

Largest numbers are found in the North Isles where there are reports throughout the year, but usually only small flocks in June and July. There is a wintering population in these islands of up to 800 birds. Main spring passage is in May and in autumn between July and October.

### SEMIPALMATED SANDPIPER *Calidris pusilla*

Very rare

3 records : 1 on Stronsay on 7th and 8th June 1993, 1 at Eve's Howe, Deerness on 25th July 1997 and 1 at Loch of Tankerness on 28th and 29th June 2002.

### WESTERN SANDPIPER *Calidris mauri*

Very rare

The only record is of a juvenile at Eve's Howe, Deerness from 28th September to 1st October 1998.

### LITTLE STINT *Calidris minuta*

Uncommon passage visitor, more numerous in autumn

An irregular spring migrant. Apart from 2 on 8th March there are records involving 1-3 birds between 8th May and 29th June. The autumn extreme dates are 15th July and 25th October, with the majority of records in August and September and a maximum of 52 on North Ronaldsay on 7th September 1998.

## TEMMINCK'S STINT *Calidris temminckii*

Very rare

There are 8 records in spring with extreme dates 8th May to 30th June. Two autumn records on 28th July and 6th September. All are of single birds.

## WHITE-RUMPED SANDPIPER *Calidris fuscicollis*

Very rare

There are 13 records, all of single birds : July - 3, September - 3, October - 6 and November - 1. Extreme dates of 22nd July and 17th November.

## BAIRD'S SANDPIPER Calidris bairdii

Very rare

The only record is of 1 on North Ronaldsay from 4th to 11th October 1993.

## PECTORAL SANDPIPER *Calidris melanotos*

Rare visitor, most often recorded in autumn

Sightings have involved 1-3 birds. Spring records have been between 6th May and 25th June. In autumn most records have been in August and September, with extreme dates of 5th July and 11th October.

## CURLEW SANDPIPER *Calidris ferruginea*

Uncommon passage visitor, more numerous in autumn

In spring rather irregular, recorded between 5th May and 23rd June and only in small numbers, usually involving 1-6 birds. Autumn records have been between 5th July and 9th November, with the majority of sightings in August and September. The highest count is 59 on North Ronaldsay on 27th August 1988 but most reports are of 1-10 birds.

## PURPLE SANDPIPER *Calidris maritima*

Common passage and winter visitor, a few birds may be present in summer

Photo: Rod Thorne

The winter population has been estimated to be over 5,500 birds. The majority have left by the end of May and the first returning birds arrive in July, although numbers in the autumn do not really increase until October.

## DUNLIN (Plover page) *Calidris alpina*

Fairly common but localised breeding species; common on passage and in winter

Has declined as a breeding species in the last 100 years due to loss of habitat, with main breeding populations on Hoy and Mainland. The wintering population is estimated at over 2,000 and flocks of 500 birds have been reported from suitable localities. Passage noticeable in May and again from July through to October.

Photo: Stuart Williams

**BROAD-BILLED SANDPIPER** *Limicola falcinellus* Very rare

2 records of single birds : 8th-10th June 1985 at Brodgar, Stenness and 9th June 1999 at Loch of Tankerness.

**BUFF-BREASTED SANDPIPER** *Tryngites subruficollis* Very rare

Between 1976 and 2003 there were 13 records, all of single birds with, in spring, 3 between 21st May and 26th June and, in autumn, 10 between 3rd September and 11th October.

Photo ©Rod Thorne

**RUFF** *Philomachus pugnax*

Fairly common passage visitor, most numerous in autumn with occasional records in winter and mid-summer

The main spring passage is in April and May and, in autumn, August and September. Most reports involve 1-40 birds but 127 were recorded in Deerness on 4th September 1997. In recent years a small flock, maximum 18, has been present in the Toab area during the winter.

**JACK SNIPE** *Lymnocryptes minimus* Uncommon passage and winter visitor; not recorded in June and July

Small numbers present in winter with spring passage from February to May, sightings usually of 1-2 birds. The main autumn passage is from September to November, with most reports involving 1-6 birds, but 45 were recorded on North Ronaldsay on 3rd October 1995.

**SNIPE (Horse gowk)** *Gallinago gallinago* Common breeding species; common on passage and in winter

A widespread breeding species, particularly in marshland and moorland. There is a noticeable increase in numbers in autumn from August through to October, when counts of 100-500 may be reported.

**GREAT SNIPE** *Gallinago media* Rare

There are several 19th century and early 20th century records. More recently between 1989 and 2004 there are 16 records, all of single birds : May - 2, August - 2, September - 6 and October - 6.

**LONG-BILLED DOWITCHER** *Limnodromus scolopaceus* Very rare

There are 5 records, all since 1983, involving single birds : 1 in September and 4 in October between 24th September and 27th October.

**DOWITCHER** sp. *Limnodromus scolopaceus or L. griseus* Very rare

A dowitcher, not specifically identified, was seen on North Ronaldsay on 4th April 1970.

**WOODCOCK** *Scolopax rusticola* Uncommon passage migrant and winter visitor; has bred

There are 2 breeding records from the 19th century. A nest was found in 1923 and injury-feigning birds noted in suitable habitat in 1963 and 1984. Winters in small numbers, usually 1-6 birds, but there were up to 100 present in the north east of Hoy in January 1985. Spring passage occurs in April, but the main influxes are in the autumn from mid-October through to December, when birds are reported from throughout the islands.

**BLACK-TAILED GODWIT** *Limosa limosa* A rare breeding species and fairly common passage visitor, particularly in the autumn, occasionally birds present mid-winter

First confirmed breeding was in 1956. Rather irregular at first, but in recent years up to 5 pairs have been recorded annually. Main passage in spring is in April and May and in autumn during August and September, with a maximum count of 130 at Mill Dam, Shapinsay on 31st August 2002.

Photo Chris Booth

## BAR-TAILED GODWIT (Tang whaup) *Limosa lapponica*

Fairly common winter and passage visitor

Photo ©Rod Thorne

Recorded throughout the year, usually frequenting sandy beaches and shores. There is a winter population of probably over 800 birds. Highest numbers are recorded in the autumn, with a maximum count of 800+ at Otterswick, Sanday on 15th August 2000. In some years up to 200 have been recorded on Sanday in mid-summer.

## WHIMBREL (Little whaup) *Numenius phaeopus*

Formerly uncommon but now rare breeding summer visitor; fairly common on passage, rare in winter

Several breeding records in the 19th century and again in the 20th century up until 1968. Since then it has bred regularly, and numbers increased to between 10 and 20 pairs. More recently there appears to have been a decline, only 5 pairs were reported in 2003 and 3 in 2004. Main spring passage is from mid-April to June and return passage in autumn from July to end of September. Occasional records November to March.

## CURLEW (Whaup) *Numenius arquata*

Common breeding species; abundant in winter

Has increased as a breeding species during the 20th century and now about 5,000 pairs breed. Very numerous in winter with an estimated population of 20,000 birds.

Photo Alan Hourston

## SPOTTED REDSHANK *Tringa erythropus*

Rare visitor in spring and usually in autumn, but in some years may be uncommon. Rare in winter

Spring passage of 1-2 birds noted between 26th March and 27th June and in autumn of 1-14 birds from 12th July to 14th November. Overwintering birds have been recorded and there are occasional reports in January, February and December.

**REDSHANK** *Tringa totanus* Fairly common breeding species; common on passage and in winter

Well distributed in marshland areas as a breeding bird with over 1,500 pairs throughout the islands. In winter the population has been estimated at 7,000 birds. Passage is noticeable March and April and again July-September.

**MARSH SANDPIPER** *Tringa stagnatilis* Very rare

The only record is of a single bird on North Ronaldsay on 23rd August 1979.

**GREENSHANK** *Tringa nebularia* An uncommon passage migrant in spring and autumn, very rare in winter; has bred

The only breeding records were in 1926 and 1951. Passage recorded in spring from 8th March to 1st July, with the majority of records in April and May. Autumn passage from 8th July to 25th November, and most numerous in August and September. There was a maximum count of 14 on North Ronaldsay on 12th August 1980. Occasional records in January, February and December.

**LESSER YELLOWLEGS** *Tringa flavipes* Very rare

There are 3 records : a juvenile at Loch of Tankerness on 15th September 1991, 1 on 26th Oct. 1999 Birsay Bay and 1 Loch of Tankerness 3rd-4th September 2003

**GREEN SANDPIPER** *Tringa ochropus* Uncommon passage visitor, most numerous in the autumn. Very rare in winter

In spring, recorded from 30th March to 22nd June, with the majority of reports in May. Autumn passage noted from 2nd July to 4th November and most numerous in August and the first 2 weeks of September. The maximum count is 9 on North Ronaldsay on 2nd September 1988. There is 1 record of a bird probably overwintering.

**WOOD SANDPIPER** *Tringa glareola* Mainly a rare passage visitor in spring and autumn but in some years uncommon. Very rare in winter

Spring records are between 30th April and 1st July and in autumn from 20th July to 17th November. The majority of records are of single birds but occasionally sightings of 2 and 3 birds are reported. There is 1 December record.

**TEREK SANDPIPER** *Xenus cinereus* Very rare

A bird was present at the Loch of Tankerness from 5th to 8th June 1987. This is the only record.

**COMMON SANDPIPER (Boondie)** *Actitis hypoleucos* Uncommon breeding species; uncommon on passage

Since 1973 there have been breeding reports from Hoy, Mainland and Rousay, with probably between 10 and 20 pairs attempting to breed annually. Apart from an early bird on 21st March, extreme passage dates are 18th April and 26th October, with a late bird seen on 19th December.

**SPOTTED SANDPIPER** *Actitis macularius* Very rare

There is just 1 record, that of a single bird seen on Sule Skerry from 30th July to 4th August 1983.

## TURNSTONE (Stoney putter) *Arenaria interpres*

Common winter and passage visitor, recorded throughout the year, but only small numbers present mid-summer

Photo ©Stuart Williams

There have been reports of birds on territory and displaying during summer on several occasions from the North Isles but, as yet, there has been no confirmation of nesting. The winter population has been estimated at about 6,000 birds. Spring passage occurs in April and May and return passage from July through to October.

## WILSON'S PHALAROPE *Phalaropus tricolor*

Very rare

There are only 2 records, both of single birds : Birsay on 3rd September 1981 and Loch of Tankerness 5th September 2002.

## RED-NECKED PHALAROPE *Phalaropus lobatus*

A regular but rare summer visitor, formerly bred

Photo ©Stuart Williams

A few pairs may have bred in the first half of the 20th century with the last report of possible breeding in 1972. Has been recorded in most years since 1986 with a maximum count of 6 on North Ronaldsay on 25th May 1999. Extreme dates are 22nd May and 22nd September.

## GREY PHALAROPE *Phalaropus fulicarius*

Mainly a rare autumn and winter visitor, very rare at other times

Recorded in every month except April, but the majority of reports have been in the months September to November, with most sightings in September. Reports usually involve single birds but 15 were recorded on North Ronaldsay on 10th September 1977 and 11 there on 16th September 1992.

# SKUAS : Stercorariidae

## POMARINE SKUA *Stercorarius pomarinus*

Uncommon passage visitor most numerous in autumn

The extreme dates in spring are 24th April and 20th June with most reports in May. The main autumn passage is from August to November with extreme dates 1st July and 22nd December. There is 1 January record.

## ARCTIC SKUA (Skootie allan) *Stercorarius parasiticus*

Common breeding summer visitor and passage migrant

Photo ©Ian Hourston

Has increased as a breeding species during the 20th century and 1,056 apparently occupied territories were found in the 1992 survey. Since then numbers have decreased and only 720 apparently occupied territories were counted in the Seabird

Photo ©Chris Booth

2000 census. One of the reasons for this decrease may be the predation of young by Great Skuas.

There is a sighting on 15th March, otherwise earliest arrival date is 9th April and the majority of birds have left by the end of September, with occasional sightings in October and November. The latest record is on 4th December.

Photo ©P & V Reynolds

**LONG-TAILED SKUA** *Stercorarius longicaudus*

An uncommon passage visitor in spring and autumn but numbers fluctuate and in some years may be rare and in others fairly common. Occasionally birds are present mid-summer

The earliest spring date is 4th May and the latest, in autumn, is 30th November. Highest passage count in 1 day is 66 off North Ronaldsay on 8th September 1991.

Photo ©Chris Booth

**GREAT SKUA (Bonxie)** *Catharacta skua*

Common breeding summer resident; common on passage. Rare in winter

There was an increase from 2 breeding pairs in 1915 to a count of 2,209 apparently occupied territories in the the Seabird 2000 census. Numbers of breeding pairs at some colonies, particularly on Hoy, have since declined.

There are occasional reports in January and February, but first birds arrive on their breeding grounds at the end of March. Most have left by the end of September, though sightings continue into November and sometimes December.

## GULLS : Laridae

**MEDITERRANEAN GULL** *Larus melanocephalus* — Very rare

There was an adult on Stronsay on 22nd and 23rd September 1996. From 1998-2003 an adult has been seen annually on North Ronaldsay and probably this was the same bird which was seen on Stronsay in September 1998 and October 1999. An adult was seen on Shapinsay 9th April 2001 and a 1st winter bird at Finstown from 24th November 2002 to 23rd March 2003. There were records of 2 other birds on North Ronaldsay in 2003. In 2004 a single bird was seen on 19th and 20th September and another on 9th October.

**LAUGHING GULL** *Larus atricilla* — Very rare

The only record is of an adult in Stenness from 16th-22nd May 1991.

**LITTLE GULL** *Larus minutus* — Uncommon passage visitor but rather irregular and in some years may be rare

Recorded in all months but most frequently in May and June and August to October.

**SABINE'S GULL** *Larus sabini* — Rare visitor most numerous in the autumn

This species was first recorded in 1975. It is an irregular visitor with only 2 spring records, both in May; all other sightings have been in autumn between late July and 1st November with July - 1, August - 6, September - 17, October - 11 and November - 1.

## BLACK-HEADED GULL (Rittock) *Larus ridibundus*

Common breeding species, passage and winter visitor

2,854 apparently occupied nests were found during the Seabird 2000 census. Fewer birds are present in mid-winter with numbers increasing from mid-February.

## RING-BILLED GULL *Larus delawarensis*

Rare winter visitor, very rare at other times

No records prior to 1983. Has been recorded annually since 1988 but most sightings refer to the same bird returning in subsequent winters. Wintering birds are present to mid-March and occasionally to June. There are 2 September records; date of earliest winter sighting is 26th November.

## COMMON GULL (Whitemaa) *Larus canus*

Common breeding species; abundant on passage and in winter

The commonest of the breeding gulls in Orkney with 11,141 apparently occupied nests found in the Seabird 2000 census. Flocks of up to 2,000 birds are not infrequent in spring and autumn.

## LESSER BLACK-BACKED GULL *Larus fuscus*

Common breeding summer visitor; very rare in winter

A total of approximately 1,600 breeding pairs was found in the 1985-87 survey, but numbers at some colonies have declined since then and only 1,045 apparently occupied nest sites were counted in the Seabird 2000 census. First returning birds are noted in mid-February and most have left by the end of September.

Birds of the races *L.f.fuscus* and *L.f.intermedius* occasionally reported.

## HERRING GULL (Whitemaa) *Larus argentatus*

Common breeding resident and winter visitor

There has been a decline at some colonies since the survey in 1985-1987 when the population was estimated at over 2,700 breeding pairs. The Seabird 2000 census found 1,933 apparently occupied nests. Breeds both at coastal and inland sites.

## Yellow-legged Herring Gull *Larus argentatus cachinnans/ michahellis*

Very rare

There are 7 records of birds belonging to one of these races : 1 in April 1989, 3 in July 1995, singles in March 1997, 18th June 1998 and 2nd September 1999.

## ICELAND GULL *Larus glaucoides*

Usually an uncommon winter and spring visitor but in some years may be rare

Most frequent from October to June, rare from July to the end of September. The majority of sightings involve 1 to 3 birds but up to 12 have been reported from Stromness Harbour and 10 from Kirkwall Harbour.

## Kumlein's Gull *Larus g. kumleini*

Very rare

There is 1 record of this North American race, a bird found dead on North Ronaldsay on 27th January 1993.

## GLAUCOUS GULL *Larus hyperboreus*

Uncommon winter visitor

Has been recorded in every month, but is most numerous from January to May and then October to December.

Photo © Chris Booth

## GREAT BLACK-BACKED GULL (Baakie, Swartback)

*Larus marinus*

Common breeding resident

The breeding population was estimated at over 5,700 pairs in 1985-87 survey. There has been a decline at some of the larger colonies, especially on Hoy, during the last 10 years. The Seabird 2000 census counted 5,505 apparently occupied nest sites.

## ROSS'S GULL *Rhodostethia rosea*

Very rare

All records are of single birds in 1997 : North Ronaldsay on 2nd October and 16th November and at Point of Ayre, Deerness on 22nd November.

Photo © Chris Booth

## KITTIWAKE (Kittick) *Rissa tridactyla*

Abundant breeding summer visitor and passage migrant; uncommon in winter

Although still abundant as a breeding species, the count of 64,000 pairs in the 1985-87 survey showed a decline from the survey of 1969-70. The decline continues in some colonies with only 57,664 apparently occupied nest sites found in the Seabird 2000 census.

## IVORY GULL *Pagophila eburnea*

Rare visitor

There are no recent records but at least 11 records between 1832 and 1949, with dated ones in the following months : February - 1, April to May - 4, November - 2, December - 2.

# TERNS : Sternidae

## GULL-BILLED TERN *Sterna nilotica*

Very rare

Only 2 records : 1 on Pentland Skerries on 7th May 1913 and 1 on North Ronaldsay on 27th May 1992.

## CASPIAN TERN *Sterna caspia*

Very rare

The only record is of 1 on Papa Westray on 16th April 1998

## SANDWICH TERN *Sterna sandvicensis*

Fairly common breeding summer visitor, very rare in winter

The number of breeding birds fluctuates, although the population for many years was usually about 300 pairs. The 1994 survey counted 566 adults in 5 colonies. In the Seabird 2000 census only 173 apparently occupied nests were found. Location of nesting colonies may also vary although some sites are occupied fairly regularly. Wintering birds have been recorded, but generally first birds arrive in late March and last ones are seen in mid-October.

## ROSEATE TERN *Sterna dougallii*

Rare summer visitor

In 1969 up to 3 pairs were seen carrying fish and displaying in an Arctic Tern colony on Sanday, but breeding was not confirmed. Since then there have only been 9 records, all occurring between 5th May and 27th July.

## COMMON TERN (Pickie-terno or Ritto) *Sterna hirundo*

Fairly common breeding summer visitor

Numbers of breeding birds fluctuate, often the colonies may be associated with those of Arctic Terns. A survey in 1994 found 374 birds in 17 colonies, while in 1980 there were 300 birds in 28 colonies but only 125 apparently occupied nests were found in the Seabird 2000 census.

## ARCTIC TERN *Sterna paradisaea*

Abundant but declining breeding summer visitor

Photo ©Ian Hourston

A survey in 1994 found 16,039 birds in 209 colonies, a decrease of 62% from the 1980 survey. 13,476 apparently occupied nests were counted in the Seabird 2000 census. Breeding success has often been poor in recent years with lack of food, such as sandeels, and unfavourable weather conditions, being some of the main factors affecting colonies. Extreme dates are 2nd April and 16th November.

## FORSTER'S TERN *Sterna forsteri*

Very rare

1 in the Eynhallow/Gairsay Sounds area 24th-27th October 2001

## BRIDLED TERN *Sterna anaethetus*

Very rare

An immature bird in Stromness 6th-7th August 1979 is the only record.

## LITTLE TERN *Sterna albifrons*

Rare summer visitor and breeding species

Has been an almost annual visitor since 1981 with extreme dates 5th May and 4th October. The first breeding record was in 1984 but breeding was not recorded again until 1997. Since then up to 5 pairs have attempted to breed annually.

## BLACK TERN *Chlidonias niger*

Rare and irregular passage visitor

Not recorded every year. Sightings have involved 1-4 birds with extreme dates 22nd April and 26th October.

## WHITE-WINGED BLACK TERN *Chlidonias leucopterus*

Very rare

There are 12 records, all between 1966 and 2004 and all of single birds. Most frequently recorded in June and July, with extreme dates 24th May and 21st November.

# AUKS : Alcidae

## GUILLEMOT (Aak) *Uria aalge*

Abundant breeding species, common in winter and on passage

Photo ©P & V Reynolds

The largest colonies are found on the west coast of Westray, on Copinsay and at Marwick Head. The Seabird 2000 census count was 181,026 birds. Occasionally "wrecks" occur during the winter following periods of strong onshore winds.

**BRÜNNICH'S GUILLEMOT** *Uria lomvia* Very rare

There are 7 records, 6 of which are of birds found dead in the following months : January - 2, March - 1, April - 1 and December - 2. The only sighting of a live bird was from Sule Skerry on 25th January 1991.

Photo © Chris Booth

**RAZORBILL** **(Coulterneb)** *Alca torda*
Common breeding species; uncommon in winter

The Seabird 2000 census found 10,194 birds, with Mainland and Westray having some of the largest numbers.

**GREAT AUK** *Pinguinus impennis* **Extinct**

The last birds in Orkney were killed in 1812 and 1813 on Papa Westray.

Photo © Alan Hourston

**BLACK GUILLEMOT** **(Tystie)** *Cepphus grylle*
Common resident breeding species

Just under 6,900 birds were counted in the 1985-87 survey, but since then numbers at some colonies appear to have declined and 5,812 birds were found in the Seabird 2000 census.
Largest colonies occur on rat-free islands.

**LITTLE AUK** **(Rotchie)** *Alle alle* Usually an uncommon winter and passage visitor but numbers can vary considerably, ranging from rare to common. Very rare in summer

Apart from 3 records in July, extreme dates are 24th August and 30th April, but the majority of records are from October to March. Passage movements involving hundreds of birds have been recorded.

Photo © Chris Booth

**PUFFIN** **(Tammie norrie)** *Fratercula arctica*
Abundant but localised breeding species; usually rare in winter

The Seabird 2000 census found 61,758 apparently occupied burrows. The main breeding colony is on Sule Skerry with 59,471 apparently occupied burrows. Smaller colonies are found on Hoy, Westray and offshore islands such as Auskerry, Pentland Skerries and Swona but groups of 1-5 birds may be seen on many cliffs in the breeding season.

## SANDGROUSE : Pteroclididae

**PALLAS'S SANDGROUSE** *Syrrhaptes paradoxus* Very rare

The only records are from the 19th century, in 1863 and in 1888, when a large scale irruption occurred.

## PIGEONS and DOVES : Columbidae

### ROCK DOVE (Doo) *Columba livia*
Common breeding resident

Well distributed throughout the islands, there has been interbreeding with feral birds.

### STOCK DOVE *Columba oenas*
Rare passage visitor, very rare in winter

This species was very rare until 1991 but has been recorded annually in small numbers since then. In spring most records are in April with extreme dates 2nd March and 17th June, with sightings involving 1-3 birds. Autumn records are of single birds between 31st August and 12th November.

### WOOD PIGEON *Columba palumbus*
Fairly common resident breeding species and uncommon passage visitor

Photo ©Chris Booth

Breeding has been reported from Eday, Hoy, Mainland, Papa Westray, Rousay and Westray, but is probably under-recorded. As well as in trees and bushes, nests may also be found on the ground in heather and juncus. Passage has been noted annually involving small numbers of birds, in spring from March to June and in autumn from July to November. Flocks of over 100 birds have been recorded from September to December.

### COLLARED DOVE *Streptopelia decaocto*
Uncommon breeding resident and passage visitor

Photo ©Chris Booth

This species was first recorded in Orkney in 1962 and breeding confirmed in 1964. It is now well established in small numbers around gardens and farm buildings, particularly on Mainland. Passage noted regularly, both in spring and autumn, with highest numbers recorded in May.

### TURTLE DOVE *Streptopelia turtur*
Uncommon but regular passage visitor

Recorded regularly in small numbers with main passage movements in May and again in September. Extreme dates are 28th April and 10th November.

### RUFOUS TURTLE DOVE *Streptopelia orientalis*
Very rare

There is just 1 record, that of a 1st winter bird present in Stromness from 20th November to 20th December 2002.

Photo ©Stuart Williams

## CUCKOOS : Cuculidae

### GREAT SPOTTED CUCKOO *Clamator glandarius*
Very rare

The only record is of an immature bird in Rendall from 14th-30th August 1959.

### CUCKOO (Gowk) *Cuculus canorus*
Uncommon passage visitor; occasionally breeds

Although juvenile birds are reported during most years, the last confirmed breeding was in 2001. A regular passage migrant in small numbers, most frequent May and June, with extreme dates of 27th April and 29th September.

## YELLOW-BILLED CUCKOO *Coccyzus americanus*

Very rare

There are 3 records of this American species, all of single birds : Birsay on 22nd October 1936, Sandwick on 12th October 1956 and North Ronaldsay on 25th September 1991.

### BARN OWLS : Tytonidae

## BARN OWL *Tyto alba*

Very rare

There are 10 records of single birds, all between 1900 and 2004. 8 were identified as belonging to the dark-breasted form *T.a.guttata.* Distribution of records : February - 2, May - 1, August - 2, October - 1, November - 3. There is 1 record of the British race *T.a.alba* in September 2003.

### OWLS : Strigidae

## SCOPS OWL *Otus scops*

Very rare

There are 7 records, all of single birds : April - 1, June - 4, October - 1 and November - 1.

## SNOWY OWL *Bubo scandiaca*

A rare and irregular passage visitor most numerous in spring

No recent records, the last sighting was in 1996. In spring the majority of reports have been in May and June, although there are records from February to July. The earliest date in autumn is 8th October. A pair summered in 1963.

## LONG-EARED OWL *Asio otus*

Uncommon passage and winter visitor; occasional birds present in summer; has bred

Although birds have been recorded during the summer in recent years, the only confirmed breeding attempts since 1971 have been in 1997 and 2004. In winter, communal roosts occur in suitable localities such as plantations or groups of bushes, with up to 25 birds having been recorded in a single roost. The majority of wintering birds have left by the end of March and, in autumn, first birds may arrive in September, but the main influx is from mid-October.

## SHORT-EARED OWL (Cattie face) *Asio flammeus*

Uncommon resident breeding species and passage migrant

Breeding pairs have been found on Eday, Hoy, Mainland, Rousay, Sanday, South Ronaldsay and Stronsay, with the highest number on Mainland. There are few sightings in mid-winter with an increase from the end of February, then declining in October.

## TENGMALM'S OWL *Aegolius funereus*

Very rare

There are 5 records, all since 1959 : May and June - 3, October-January - 2.

## NIGHTJARS : Caprimulgidae

### NIGHTJAR *Caprimulgus europaeus*

Rare visitor, most numerous in spring

Apart from an April record in 1868, all spring sightings have been between 6th May and 15th June. There are only 3 autumn records, 2 in September, the other on 2nd October. About 18 individuals have been recorded since 1900.

### COMMON NIGHTHAWK *Chordeiles minor*

Very rare

1 trapped at Wideford Burn, St Ola on 12th September 1978 is the only record of this American species.

## SWIFTS : Apodidae

### NEEDLE-TAILED SWIFT *Hirundapus caudacutus*

Very rare

There are just 2 records, both of single birds : At Windwick, South Ronaldsay on 11th and 12th June 1983 and Melsetter, Hoy from 28th May to 8th June 1988.

### SWIFT *Apus apus*

Often an uncommon passage visitor but in some years may be fairly common

Most often recorded from June to August with sightings usually involving 1-6 birds, but flocks of up to 150 have been reported. Extreme dates are 22nd April and 30th November.

### PALLID SWIFT *Apus pallidus*

Very rare

An adult found moribund at the lighthouse, North Ronaldsay on 26th October 1996 is the only record.

### ALPINE SWIFT *Apus melba*

Very rare

There are 2 records, both from North Ronaldsay and of single birds on 8th June 1965 and 12th August 1988.

## KINGFISHERS : Alcedinidae

### KINGFISHER *Alcedo atthis*

Very rare

There have been only 4 records during the period 1972 to 2004 and in the following months : April - 2, July - 1 and November - 1.

## BEE-EATERS : Meropidae

### BEE-EATER *Merops apiaster*

Very rare visitor

The first record was of 3 from 31st May to 5th June 1966, since then a minimum of 15 individuals has been recorded, with extreme dates 17th May and 18th September.

## ROLLERS : Coraciidae

### ROLLER *Coracias garrulus*

Very rare visitor

There are a number of 19th century records but only 4 since 1900, all of single birds in May 1937, July 1950, May to July 1958 and June 1966.

## HOOPOES : Upupidae

### HOOPOE *Upupa epops*

Rare visitor

A regular passage visitor but usually only 1-3 are reported annually and slightly more numerous in autumn. In spring, recorded between 3rd April and 21st June and, in autumn, between 22nd August and 17th November.

## WOODPECKERS : Picidae

### WRYNECK *Jynx torquilla*

A passage visitor in spring and autumn in varying numbers. In some years is uncommon and in others rare

In spring, recorded between 20th April and 6th June. Usually more numerous in autumn with records between 14th August and 17th October. The highest count was 30 on North Ronaldsay on 2nd September 1988.

### GREEN WOODPECKER *Picus viridis*

Very rare

There is a 19th century record of a bird seen in Kirkwall in July 1885.

### GREAT SPOTTED WOODPECKER *Dendrocopos major*

An irregular and irruptive passage visitor in autumn in varying numbers, has overwintered. Rare on spring passage and very rare in summer

In spring there are records of single passage birds between 30th March and 30th May. In June and July 1976 1 was present in Trumland Woods, Rousay. Earliest autumn date is 13th August but most records are from the end of this month until the end of October, with fewer in November and December. There are several records of birds overwintering.

## LARKS : Alaudidae

### CALANDRA LARK *Melanocorypha calandra*

Very rare

1 on North Ronaldsay on 10th and 11th May 2002 is the only record

### SHORT-TOED LARK *Calandrella brachydactyla*

Rare passage visitor most numerous in autumn

This species has been recorded in all but 5 of the years between 1987 and 2004. In spring, records are between 24th April and 9th June and, in autumn, between 29th August and 20th October.

### WOODLARK *Lullula arborea*

Very rare

There are 7 records in the following months: March - 2, October - 4, October and November - 1. 4 of these were between 1911 and 1913 and there were singles in 1988, 1993 and 1998.

Photo ©Stuart Williams

### SKYLARK (Laverock or Lavero) *Alauda arvensis*

Common breeding species and passage visitor; fairly common in winter

Although widespread as a breeding bird, numbers probably declined during the 20th century. Spring passage occurs from late February through to April and in autumn the main passage is in September and October.

### SHORE LARK *Eremophila alpestris*

An irregular passage visitor usually rare but occasionally uncommon

Has been recorded in winter and spring between 5th February and 3rd June and, in autumn, between 18th September and 5th December. Sightings have been mainly of 1-3 birds, but there was an exceptional influx in 1976 when there was a maximum count of 60 on North Ronaldsay on 6th October.

## MARTINS and SWALLOWS : Hirundinidae

### SAND MARTIN (Witchuck) *Riparia riparia*

A regular passage migrant usually uncommon, but numbers vary ranging from rare in some years to fairly common in others; rare breeding species

Most numerous in May with a few mid-summer records and the main autumn passage in September. The earliest date is 27th March and latest 16th October. There were occasional breeding records prior to 1943 but no more until 2001, 2002, 2003 and 2004.

### CRAG MARTIN *Ptyonoprogne rupestris*

Very rare

The only record is of 1 seen near Finstown on 3rd May 1999.

### SWALLOW *Hirundo rustica*

Fairly common breeding summer visitor and passage migrant

The swallow has increased as a breeding species in recent years, from 64 pairs in 1987 to at least 273 pairs in 1997 and the population is now probably in excess of 300 pairs. The main passage movements are in May and again in September, the extreme dates are 9th March and 7th December. Autumn roosts of up to 2,500 birds have been recorded.

### RED-RUMPED SWALLOW *Hirundo daurica*

Very rare

There are 7 records, all of single birds. In spring there are 5 records between 4th May and 16th June and 2 autumn records on 7th and 18th October.

### HOUSE MARTIN *Delichon urbicum*

Formerly rare breeding summer visitor, now uncommon; uncommon on passage

Breeding of this species has been recorded annually between 1983 and 2000 but only in small numbers with a maximum of 10 pairs. However, since 2001, probably helped by the provision of artificial nest boxes, numbers have increased and at least 30 nests were reported in 2003 and also in 2004. It is most numerous on spring passage, particularly during May and June, with fewer reported in autumn. Extreme dates 4th April and 10th November.

## PIPITS and WAGTAILS : Motacillidae

### RICHARD'S PIPIT *Anthus novaeseelandiae*

Very rare visitor in winter and spring; regular but rare on passage in autumn

There are records of single birds on 20th January 2000 and 13th April 1967. In autumn it has been recorded between 10th September and 3rd November. A flock of 7 was present on North Ronaldsay on 27th September 1992.

### TAWNY PIPIT *Anthus campestris*

Very rare

There are 2 records, both of single birds, on Stronsay on 27th and 28th May 1988 and on Papa Westray on 29th May 1998.

### OLIVE-BACKED PIPIT *Anthus hodgsoni*

Rare and irregular autumn visitor

Apart from 2 seen on 28th September 2001, all other records are of single birds with extreme dates 24th September and 6th Nov.

### TREE PIPIT *Anthus trivialis*

Fairly common passage migrant with sometimes large numbers in May

Extreme dates in spring are 18th April and 28th June and in autumn 9th August and 11th November.

### PECHORA PIPIT *Anthus gustavi*

Very rare

The only record is of a single bird on North Ronaldsay on 3rd October 1989.

### MEADOW PIPIT (Teeting) *Anthus pratensis*

Abundant breeding summer visitor, uncommon in winter

Widespread as a breeding species. The first returning birds in spring are usually noted about the 3rd week of March and the main autumn passage occurs in late August and during September, with few birds remaining after the end of October.

### RED-THROATED PIPIT *Anthus cervinus*

Rare visitor

In spring there are 7 records between 7th May and 4th June and, in autumn, 10 records between 11th September and 27th October.

### ROCK PIPIT (Tang sparrow) *Anthus petrosus*

Fairly common resident breeding species and passage visitor

Breeding pairs are well distributed around the coasts of all the islands. Passage movements have been recorded in March and April and then again during September and October. In winter small numbers can be found at inland, mainly moorland, sites.

### Scandinavian Rock Pipit *A.p.littoralis*

Very rare

Birds of this race have been recorded in spring in 1912, 1992, 1996 and 1998-2001. 1 was seen in August 1999

### WATER PIPIT *Anthus spinoletta*

Very rare

There are 2 records of single birds : 13th April 1991 and 7th May 1996.

### YELLOW WAGTAIL *Motacilla flava*

A passage visitor which may be uncommon in some years and rare in others; has bred

Breeding was confirmed on Papa Westray in 1979 and a pair probably bred on Westray in 1980. Spring passage has been noted between 1st April and 21st July, with the majority of sightings in May and in autumn from 30th July to 13th November it being most numerous in September. Birds of the races *M.f.flava, M.f. flassima* and *M.f.thunbergi* have been specifically identified on a number of occasions in both spring and autumn.

### CITRINE WAGTAIL *Motacilla citreola*

Very rare

There are 9 records, all of single birds and occurring between 26th August and 11th October.

### GREY WAGTAIL *Motacilla cinerea*

A rare and irregular breeding species; uncommon passage migrant and rare winter visitor

There are occasional breeding records prior to 1974. Between 1976 and 2004 breeding has been confirmed in 13 years involving 1-3 pairs. Passage is most evident during March, April, September and October with fewer reports at other times; overwintering has been recorded.

## PIED/WHITE WAGTAIL (Willie wagtail) *Motacilla alba*

### Pied Wagtail *M.a.yarrellii*

Fairly common breeding summer visitor and passage migrant; rare in winter

Has increased as a breeding species in the last 30 years and it is now widespread throughout the islands. The first returning birds arrive in mid-March, with passage movements continuing into May. In autumn the main passage is in August and September with most birds having left by the end of October. A few birds remain in suitable localities throughout the winter.

### White Wagtail *M.a.alba*

Uncommon passage migrant; has bred

The main passage occurs in April, May and then August and September. Mixed pairing with *M.a.yarrelli* has been recorded.

**WAXWINGS : Bombycillidae**

## WAXWING *Bombycilla garrulus*

An irruptive passage visitor

Photo ©Chris Booth

This species is rare and irregular in spring while in autumn numbers vary, ranging from rare to fairly common and in some years birds may remain into February. Influxes can occur at any time from late October through to January.

**DIPPERS : Cinclidae**

## DIPPER *Cinclus cinclus*

Rare visitor; very rare and irregular breeding species

A pair bred in 1994, the first confirmed breeding since 1940. There have been occasional sightings of single birds, particularly since 1990, with at least 1 record of overwintering. Some of these sightings have been of birds identified as belonging to the British race *C.c.gularis.*

### Black-bellied Dipper *C.c.cinclus*

Very rare

A bird of this race was seen on North Ronaldsay on 4th April 1965.

**WRENS : Troglodytidae**

## WREN (Jenny wren) *Troglodytes troglodytes*

Common resident breeding species, uncommon passage visitor

Widespread as a breeding species, but numbers tend to decline after hard winters. Passage has been noted, both in spring and autumn, particularly on North Ronaldsay.

**ACCENTORS : Prunellidae**

## DUNNOCK *Prunella modularis*

Uncommon breeding resident; passage numbers vary from uncommon to fairly common

Photo ©Chris Booth

Small numbers breed in suitable habitats such as gardens and plantations. Spring passage has been noted between 17th March and 17th June and in autumn from 1st September to 30th November.

**ROBINS, CHATS and THRUSHES : Turdidae**

## ROBIN (Robin redbreast) *Erithacus rubecula*

Uncommon breeding resident and winter visitor; usually fairly common on passage but occasionally large influxes occur

Photo© Chris Booth

The majority of breeding birds are found in the Hoy plantations, Mainland and on Rousay, with a few pairs at other sites. It is more widespread in winter with 1 or 2 birds at suitable localities throughout the islands. The main spring passage takes place in late March through to May and in autumn, during September and October.

Photo ©Stuart Williams

**THRUSH NIGHTINGALE** *Luscinia luscinia* Very rare

There are 6 records, 4 in spring between 12th and 27th May and 2 in autumn on 1st and 18th September.

**NIGHTINGALE** *Luscinia megarhynchos* Very rare

There are 10 recorded sightings, 8 in spring between 11th May and 17th June and in autumn, 2 between 17th August and 21st September.

**BLUETHROAT** *Luscinia svecica*

**Red-spotted form** *L.s.svecica* Uncommon passage migrant but numbers vary and in some years rare

Has been noted in spring from 9th May to 14th June, and in autumn from 31st August to 16th November, with the majority seen in September and early October.

**White-spotted form** *L.s.cyanecula* Very rare

3 records of single birds : 31st March 1958, 6th May 1967 and 4th November 2000.

**SIBERIAN BLUE ROBIN** *Luscinia cyane* Very rare

The only record is of a 1st year male seen on North Ronaldsay on 2nd October 2001.

**BLACK REDSTART** *Phoenicurus ochruros* Uncommon passage visitor

Spring passage has been noted between 1st March and 13th June, with the majority of sightings in April and May, although there have been 4 records in January and 1 in February. In autumn recorded from 8th August to 24th December, but most numerous in last 2 weeks of October. In 1973 a female built a nest and laid eggs on Copinsay, but no male was seen.

**REDSTART** *Phoenicurus phoenicurus* Usually an uncommon passage visitor but in some years can be fairly common and very occasionally common

The main spring passage is in May, but recorded between 15th April and 26th June and single records on 3rd and 14th July. In autumn has been reported from 10th August to 17th November, with most records in September and early October.

**WHINCHAT** *Saxicola rubetra*

A fairly common passage visitor; occasional and rare breeding species

The most recent confirmed breeding record was of a pair in Rendall in 1995. Spring passage noted from 23rd March to 25th June, but peak movements are in May. Occasionally recorded in July. There are more occurrences in autumn, with passage birds reported from 9th August to 1st December with the majority occurring in September.

**STONECHAT** *Saxicola torquata*

Uncommon, occasionally fairly common, resident breeding species and passage migrant

There is a concentration of breeding pairs in Hoy and West Mainland, but numbers fluctuate due to their being affected by severe winters. Small numbers are recorded on passage in both spring (mainly March and April) and in autumn (September and October).

**Eastern Stonechat** *S.t.maura or stejnegeri*

Rare visitor

There are 17 records of birds of 1 of these races, all since 1981, with extreme dates 10th September and 23rd October.

**WHEATEAR (Stonechat, Chacko)** *Oenanthe oenanthe*

Fairly common breeding summer visitor, common on passage

This is a widespread breeding species, although in small numbers. The earliest arrival date is 10th March and latest record on 29th November. Large influxes of passage birds may occur in both spring and autumn.

**PIED WHEATEAR** *Oenanthe pleschanka*

Very rare

There are 5 records, all of single birds : 1st November 1916, 16th-20th October 1988, 22nd October 1994, 21st-24th October 1998 and 13th-27th October 2002.

**Pied Wheatear/Black-eared Wheatear** *Oenanthe pleschanka/Oenanthe hispanica*

One, not specifically identified, Deerness 16th October 1999.

Very rare

**DESERT WHEATEAR** *Oenanthe deserti*

Very rare

Recorded on 2 occasions, both single birds : 2nd June 1906 and 21st-30th October 1988.

**ROCK THRUSH** *Monticola saxatilis*

Very rare

The only record is of a male obtained on Pentland Skerries and another seen on 17th May 1910.

**WHITE'S THRUSH** *Zoothera dauma*

Very rare

There are only 2 records of this rare species. 1 was seen on Stronsay on 3rd October 1990 and 1 on North Ronaldsay from 17th-21st October 2003.

**SIBERIAN THRUSH** *Zoothera sibirica* Very rare

There are 2 records of single birds : 13th November 1984 and 1st-8th October 1992.

**SWAINSON'S THRUSH** *Catharus ustulatus* Very rare

A bird at Graemeshall, Holm on 21st October 1993 is the only record.

Photo ©Stuart Williams

**GREY-CHEEKED THRUSH** *Catharus minimus* Very rare

There are 2 records, both of single birds, on Hoy on 16th October 1994 and at Outertown, Stromness on 14th-16th October 2001.

**VEERY** *Catharus fuscescens* Very rare

The only record is of a single bird at Holland, North Ronaldsay on 30th September to 6th October 2002.

**RING OUZEL** *Turdus torquatus* Fairly common passage visitor, but in some years uncommon; very rare in winter. Rare breeding species

The last confirmed breeding was in 1977. Spring passage has been noted between 29th March and 10th June and, in autumn, from 31st August to 11th November, with majority of records in late September and in October. Occasionally recorded at other times.

Photo ©Chris Booth

**BLACKBIRD (Blackie)** *Turdus merula* Fairly common resident breeding species and winter visitor; common on passage

A widespread breeding species. The main spring passage takes place in March and April, but the highest numbers are usually recorded on autumn passage, particularly in October and early November.

**EYE-BROWED THRUSH** *Turdus obscurus* Very rare

The only record is of 1 seen in Evie on 25th and 26th September 1984.

**BLACK-THROATED THRUSH** *Turdus ruficollis* Very rare

Single birds have been recorded on 3 occasions : 26th-28th September 1990, 23rd October 1992 and 24th-27th April 1995.

**FIELDFARE** *Turdus pilaris* Common passage migrant, fairly common in winter; occasional and very rare breeding species

There are breeding records of single pairs in 1967, 1969, 1974, 1996 and 2004. Large numbers may occur on passage during spring and autumn, with main movements usually in April, October and early November.

**SONG THRUSH (Mavis)** *Turdus philomelos* Uncommon breeding resident; usually fairly common on passage and occasionally common

Widespread. There are small numbers of breeding pairs, found particularly in woods and gardens. Spring passage in March and April, but it is much more numerous on autumn passage, especially in the last week of September and during October.

**REDWING** *Turdus iliacus* — Abundant passage visitor, fairly common in winter; occasional and very rare breeding species

There are only 2 confirmed breeding attempts, in 1975 and 1993, although singing birds are reported in most years during April and May. Spring passage occurs from March to May, but numbers are not usually large; much more numerous in autumn, particularly in October and often involving thousands of birds.

**MISTLE THRUSH** *Turdus viscivorus* — Uncommon passage visitor, rare in winter; formerly a rare/uncommon breeding species

Small numbers formerly bred, particularly during the first half of the 20th century, with the last confirmed breeding being in 1971. There are occasional reports in January and February, but the main spring passage is in March and early April, with a few birds recorded in May, also sightings in June and July. Autumn passage noted from 2nd September, but majority of reports in late September, throughout October and in early November, with occasional ones in December.

**AMERICAN ROBIN** *Turdus migratorius* — Very rare

The only record is of a single bird at Kirkwall Airfield on 27th May 1961.

## WARBLERS : Sylviidae

**PALLAS'S GRASSHOPPER WARBLER** *Locustella certhiola* — Very rare

There is just 1 record, that of a bird which was trapped on North Ronaldsay. It was present there from 23rd-25th September 1992.

**LANCEOLATED WARBLER** *Locustella lanceolata* — Very rare

The only records are of single birds : On Pentland Skerries on 26th October 1910 and, in 2003, on North Ronaldsay on 8th September and on Sanday on 29th September.

**GRASSHOPPER WARBLER** *Locustella naevia* — Rare passage visitor, rather more occurrences in spring, occasionally birds heard singing up to mid-summer

Extreme dates in spring and summer are from 19th April to 24th June. It is occasionally reported in July and there is a record of a bird singing on 7th August. In autumn, recorded between 24th August and 22nd October.

**RIVER WARBLER** *Locustella fluviatilis* — Very rare

The only record is of 1 on North Ronaldsay on 15th September 1995.

**AQUATIC WARBLER** *Acrocephalus paludicola* — Very rare

The only record is of 1 on North Ronaldsay 21st and 22nd September 1999.

**SEDGE WARBLER** *Acrocephalus schoenobaenus* — Fairly common breeding summer visitor and passage migrant

A widespread breeding species in small numbers, particularly amongst rough vegetation and scrub. Extreme dates are 19th April and 13th October.

**PADDYFIELD WARBLER** *Acrocephalus agricola* — Very rare

There are 4 records of single birds : 18th July in Holm, 22nd October on Sanday and 23rd October on South Ronaldsay, all in 1994 and on 26th October on North Ronaldsay in 1997.

**BLYTH'S REED WARBLER** *Acrocephalus dumetorum* — Very rare

There are 6 records, all of single birds: Just 1 in spring, on 19th May and 5 in autumn between 22nd September and 19th October.

**MARSH WARBLER** *Acrocephalus palustris* — Rare passage visitor, most numerous in spring, and very rare breeding species

There are 2 breeding records, both of single pairs in 1993 and 1997. Spring passage has been noted between 21st May and 29th June. Apart from breeding birds there are 3 July records. In autumn, passage birds have been recorded from 24th August to 17th October.

**REED WARBLER** *Acrocephalus scirpaceus* — A passage visitor in varying numbers, being uncommon in some years and rare in others; most numerous in autumn

Spring passage recorded between 5th May and 18th June and in autumn from 9th August to 29th November, but the main passage is usually in September.

**GREAT REED WARBLER** *Acrocephalus arundinaceus* — Very rare

There are 2 records : 1 on North Ronaldsay on 11th June 1986 and 1 on Papa Westray on 29th April 1987.

**BOOTED WARBLER** *Hippolais caligata* — Very rare

2 records of single birds : On South Ronaldsay on 3rd and 4th September 1988 and on North Ronaldsay on 14th September 1993.

**SYKES'S WARBLER** *Hippolais rama* — Very rare

Just 2 records, both of single birds on North Ronaldsay, 26th August 2002 and 29th September - 1st October 2003.

**ICTERINE WARBLER** *Hippolais icterina* — Usually a rare passage visitor but in some years uncommon. Very rare breeding species

Singing birds are occasionally reported, especially in June. A pair bred in the North Isles in 2002. In spring, recorded between 3rd May and 30th June. In autumn, birds are noted between 29th July and 13th October with majority of records in August and September.

**MELODIOUS WARBLER** *Hippolais polyglotta* — Very rare

There are 13 records, all involving single birds. 4 in spring between 22nd May and 11th June and 9 in autumn between 18th August and 2nd October.

Photo ©Stuart Williams

**BLACKCAP** *Sylvia atricapilla* — A common passage migrant most numerous in autumn, occasionally winters; very rare breeding species

Only 2 confirmed breeding records, but birds have been seen on territory and breeding suspected on several occasions, including the sighting of single juveniles in July and August. In spring the earliest date is 31st March but most reports are in May, with a few sightings continuing into July. The first autumn date is 12th August, but main passage is in late September and through October, with occasional birds still present in December and rarely to March.

## GARDEN WARBLER *Sylvia borin*

A fairly common passage migrant, most numerous in autumn; very rare breeding species

Breeding has been suspected on a number of occasions but there are only 2 confirmed records. In spring the earliest date is 19th April, but most records are in May with occasional reports until mid-summer. In autumn the extreme dates are 7th August and 18th November with the main passage in September.

## BARRED WARBLER *Sylvia nisoria*

Very rare passage visitor in spring, uncommon in autumn

There are only 2 spring records : 10th May and 21st June. In autumn has been recorded between 5th August and 6th November, but most numerous in late August and in September.

Photo ©Stuart Williams

## LESSER WHITETHROAT *Sylvia curruca*

Uncommon passage visitor and very rare breeding species

The only breeding records are in 1988 and 2004, but singing birds are occasionally reported in May and June. In spring, recorded between 24th April and 18th July, with the main passage in May. In autumn, noted between 11th August and 12th November and most numerous from mid-September to mid-October. There is 1 record on 18th December. Birds showing characteristics of the Siberian race *S.c.blythii* are occasionally reported.

## WHITETHROAT *Sylvia communis*

Uncommon passage visitor and very rare breeding species

Although breeding has been suspected on a number of occasions, especially in recent years, there have only been 8 confirmed records. In spring the earliest date is 17th April, but the main passage is in May. Usually less numerous in autumn with latest date being 1st November.

## SUBALPINE WARBLER *Sylvia cantillans*

Rare visitor, most numerous in spring

16 records of single birds : 13 in spring between 9th April and 12th June. In 1999 a male was present in the Rendall area from 20th June to 16th August. Then in autumn 2 between 14th and 17th September.

## SARDINIAN WARBLER *Sylvia melanocephala*

Very rare

Recorded on 3 occasions, all single birds : Birsay 24th-27th April 1988, North Ronaldsay 25th-27th May 1992 and Stronsay 29th-31st October 1992.

## GREENISH WARBLER *Phylloscopus trochiloides*

Very rare spring visitor, rare in autumn

There are 2 spring records : 28th May 1992 and 7th June 1997, and 13 records in autumn between 14th August and 10th October.

Photo ©Stuart Williams

**ARCTIC WARBLER** *Phylloscopus borealis* — Rare visitor

There have been 20 records, all in autumn, between 15th August and 23rd September.

**PALLAS'S WARBLER** *Phylloscopus proregulus* — Rare autumn visitor

First recorded in 1982, since then there have been over 20 records, all between 11th October and 8th November.

Photo ©Rod Thorne

**YELLOW-BROWED WARBLER** *Phylloscopus inornatus* — Very rare spring visitor; usually uncommon in autumn but occasionally rare

The only spring records have been on 27th and 28th April 1995. In autumn, extreme dates are 13th September and 23rd November.

**HUME'S WARBLER** (formerly Hume's Yellow-browed Warbler) *Phylloscopus humei* — Very rare

The only record is of 1 at Cara, South Ronaldsay from 4th - 6th November 1994.

**RADDE'S WARBLER** *Phylloscopus schwarzi* — Very rare

7 records, all of single birds, between 3rd and 19th October.

**DUSKY WARBLER** *Phylloscopus fuscatus* — Very rare

7 records, all of single birds, between 1st October and 15th November.

Photo ©Stuart Williams

**WESTERN BONELLI'S WARBLER** *Phylloscopus bonelli* — Very rare

There are 3 records, all of single birds: Holm 26th October to 15th November 1986, North Ronaldsay 11th - 13th May 1994 and Herston, South Ronaldsay 29th October to 15th November 2004.

**WESTERN/EASTERN BONELLI'S WARBLER** *Phylloscopus bonelli/orientalis* — Very rare
(Species not determined)

Recorded on 3 occasions, all single birds. Spring : 17th May 1993 and 25th May 1994. Autumn : 27th September 1992.

**WOOD WARBLER** *Phylloscopus sibilatrix* — Usually an uncommon passage visitor but occasionally rare; very rare breeding species

The only breeding records were in 1914 and 1915. In spring, passage has been recorded between 3rd May and 14th June with occasional birds present in July. Extreme dates in autumn are 4th August and 1st November with main passage from mid-August to mid-September.

**CHIFFCHAFF** *Phylloscopus collybita* — Fairly common passage visitor, rare in winter; has bred

Although birds are regularly present in mid-summer and behaving as if breeding, the only confirmed breeding is that of a family party seen in Trumland Wood, Rousay on 7th August 2001. Earliest date for spring migrants is 3rd March, but main passage is in April and early May with a few birds present throughout the summer. Autumn passage starts in late August and main movements are at the end of September and throughout October. Small influxes regularly occur in early November with sightings into December and very small numbers may overwinter. Birds showing characteristics of the races *P.c.abietinus* and *P.c.tristis* have been recorded, especially in late autumn.

**WILLOW WARBLER** *Phylloscopus trochilus* — Uncommon breeding summer visitor, a fairly common and occasionally common passage visitor

Only small numbers breed, mainly confined to plantations and wooded areas. Extreme dates are 1st April and 5th November, with main passage movements in spring in May and in autumn in August and September. Occasionally falls of hundreds of birds occur at these times.

**GOLDCREST** *Regulus regulus* — Uncommon but at times rare breeding resident; common on passage, most numerous in autumn

Photo ©Rod Thorne

The majority of breeding pairs are found in the Hoy plantations and wooded areas on Mainland, with occasional breeding reports from other islands. Very small numbers are present in woods and plantations in winter. Spring passage has been noted from 9th March, with most sightings in April and a few present until late May. In autumn, occasional records in August but main movements are in late September and during October. Numbers then decline through November.

**FIRECREST** *Regulus ingnicapilla* — Rare

14 records, all of single birds. The only spring record was 2nd-3rd April, while in autumn and winter recorded between 13th September and 8th January.

## FLYCATCHERS : Muscicapidae

**SPOTTED FLYCATCHER** *Muscicapa striata* — Rare and irregular breeding summer visitor. Regular on passage with numbers varying from uncommon to fairly common and occasionally common, usually more numerous in spring

Apart from a very early record on 3rd April, the extreme passage dates are 27th April and 27th November. Between 1972 and 2004 breeding has been confirmed in 15 years, with a maximum of 3 pairs in any 1 year.

**RED-BREASTED FLYCATCHER** *Ficedula parva* — Rare but occasionally uncommon passage visitor, more numerous in autumn

Extreme dates in spring are 10th May and 16th June and in autumn 8th August and 9th December, with most sightings in October.

**COLLARED FLYCATCHER** *Ficedula albicollis* — Very rare

There are 3 records, all of single birds : Harray on 30th May 1963, Stronsay on 31st May 1980 and North Ronaldsay on 31st May 1999.

### PIED FLYCATCHER *Ficedula hypoleuca*

Regular passage visitor, in some years uncommon and in others fairly common

In spring, recorded between 24th April and 25th June, with most reports in May. There are 4 July records. Autumn sightings have been noted between 4th August and 14th November, with main passage movements in September.

## BABBLERS : Timaliidae

### BEARDED TIT *Panurus biarmicus*

Very rare

A male at Loch of Ness, Papa Westray on 13th October 1998 is the only record.

## LONG-TAILED TITS : Aegithalidae

### LONG-TAILED TIT *Aegithalos caudatus*

Rare passage visitor, very occasionally uncommon in autumn; has overwintered; very rare at other times

Apart from records of single birds on 13th May 2004 and 27th June 1974 all other sightings have been between 9th August and 2nd April, with the majority in October and November and a maximum flock size of 15. All birds critically examined have been of the British race.

## TITS : Paridae

### COAL TIT *Parus ater*

Rare visitor in the autumn, very rare at other times

There are just 2 records up until 1985. It has been more regular since then but only 1-6 birds have been recorded in any single year. The majority of sightings have been in autumn with extreme dates 21st September and 27th November and involving 1-3 birds. Other records are of 2 that were seen in Kirkwall on 13th January and 3rd February of the same year and of 1 on 22nd May.

### BLUE TIT *Parus caeruleus*

Rare visitor, has overwintered on several occasions

Apart from overwintering birds, there are records in spring from 20th March to 23rd June and in autumn from 2nd October to 28th December with a maximum of 5 birds at any one time.

### GREAT TIT *Parus major*

Rare visitor, has overwintered

There are records of birds, probably on passage, in spring from 17th March to 23rd May and in autumn from 9th September to 30th November. Sightings have involved 1-5 birds.

## TREECREEPERS : Certhiidae

### TREE CREEPER *Certhia familiaris*

Rare and irregular visitor

There are records of single birds on 9th and 10th April 2001 and 1st July 2004, otherwise recent sightings have been in autumn and winter. The majority of reports have been between 5th September and 14th November and involved single birds, but 2 have been seen on 2 occasions. There are 2 records of birds overwintering with the latest sighting on 21st February.

## ORIOLES : Oriolidae

### GOLDEN ORIOLE *Oriolus oriolus*

Rare passage visitor in spring, very rare in autumn

Has been recorded in spring from 20th April to 21st June with the majority of sightings in May and early June. There are only 4 autumn records, all between 28th July and 18th September.

## SHRIKES : Laniidae

### ISABELLINE SHRIKE *Lanius isabellinus*

Very rare visitor

There are just 3 records, all of single birds : 28th October to 2nd November 1991 on North Ronaldsay, 10th-17th September 1995 in Deerness and 30th November 1997 on North Ronaldsay.

### RED-BACKED SHRIKE *Lanius collurio*

Uncommon passage migrant usually more numerous in spring

Spring records have been between 27th April and 27th June with most sightings from mid-May to mid-June. There are 5 July records. In autumn, recorded between 3rd August and 24th October, but most numerous in September.

### LESSER GREY SHRIKE *Lanius minor*

Very rare visitor

There 3 records, all of single birds : 11th November 1962 in Finstown, 30th May 1965 on North Ronaldsay and 27th September 1967 on North Ronaldsay.

Photo ©Stuart Williams

### GREAT GREY SHRIKE *Lanius excubitor*

Regular but rare passage visitor, very occasionally uncommon, slightly more numerous in autumn

Apart from 2 birds seen on 22nd February, other spring records have been between 26th March and 25th May. 1 was seen on 5th July and then, in autumn and winter, recorded between 12th September and 17th January, with most sightings in October.

### SOUTHERN GREY SHRIKE *Lanius meridionalis*

Very rare visitor

Single birds of this race have been recorded from 14th September to 16th October on North Ronaldsay, 11th-26th November on Papa Westray, both in 1994, and 22nd September 2000 on South Ronaldsay.

### WOODCHAT SHRIKE *Lanius senator*

Very rare visitor

There are 7 spring and summer records, all involving single birds, with extreme dates 8th May and 30th June, and 2 in autumn between 18th and 26th September.

## CROWS : Corvidae

### JAY *Garrulus glandarius*

Very rare visitor

The only record is of 1 on North Ronaldsay on 11th May 1967.

### MAGPIE *Pica pica*

Very rare visitor

There are 3 records in the 19th century. Since 1900 there have been 11 records : January to May - 7, October and November - 4. Apart from 2 birds seen in 1987, all other records are of single birds.

### NUTCRACKER *Nucifraga caryocatactes*

Very rare visitor

The only record is of 1 which was shot on Sanday on 1st October 1868.

**CHOUGH** *Pyrrhocorax pyrrhocorax* — Very rare visitor

There are 5 records, all of single birds : Westray on 19th October 1935 and 14th May 1942; South Ronaldsay on 10th December 1951; Marwick Head on 6th January 1965 and 10th June 2000.

**JACKDAW** **(Jackie)** *Corvus monedula* — Fairly common breeding resident, uncommon on passage

The breeding population of this species is declining with, at present, probably less than 300 pairs. There is a very local distribution of colonies on sea cliffs on Calf of Eday, Hoy, Mainland, South Ronaldsay, Stronsay, Westray and possibly Rousay. A few pairs nest on buildings in Kirkwall and pairs may occasionally nest in trees, as at Woodwick, Evie. Small numbers (1-13) of probable migrant birds have been noted, particularly on North Ronaldsay, in spring from March to June and in autumn from September to October.

**ROOK** *Corvus frugilegus* — Common breeding resident; uncommon on passage

The last full survey was in 1996 and found a total of 1,898 nests, a 34% increase on the 1987 total of 1,419 nests. Rookeries are now confined to Mainland and Rousay, although, in the past, rooks have bred on Hoy and South Ronaldsay. Small numbers of passage birds have been reported from the outer isles in spring from March to June and in autumn from August to November.

**CARRION CROW** *Corvus corone* — Rare resident breeding species; uncommon on passage

Reports of 1 or 2 birds paired, and nesting, with Hooded Crows are received most years. Passage movements involving small numbers have been reported in spring from March to June and in autumn from August to November.

**HOODED CROW** **(Hoodie, Craa)** *Corvus cornix* — Common breeding resident and uncommon passage visitor

A widely distributed breeding species using a variety of nesting sites. Small numbers, including Carrion/Hooded hybrids, have been reported on passage from North Ronaldsay, particularly in April and May and also October.

Photo ©Chris Booth

**RAVEN** **(Corbie)** *Corvus corax* — Uncommon resident and passage visitor

A minimum of 100 nesting pairs widely distributed throughout the islands. A roost of over 100 non-breeding birds has been present in some years on Mainland. Passage has been noted on North Ronaldsay in April, May, September and October but only involving small numbers of usually less than 10 birds.

## STARLINGS : Sturnidae

Photo ©Chris Booth

**STARLING** **(Stirling, Strill)** *Sturnus vulgaris* — Common breeding resident; abundant passage and winter visitor

A widely distributed breeding species with flocks of up to 2,000 reported regularly in autumn and winter.

**ROSE-COLOURED STARLING** *Sturnus roseus* Rare visitor in summer and autumn

There have been over 20 records since 1932 involving both adult and juvenile birds. Extreme dates are 5th June and 15th November, with most sightings from June to August.

## SPARROWS : Passeridae

**HOUSE SPARROW** **(Sparrow)** *Passer domesticus* Common breeding resident

Although still a common and widely distributed species around habitation, especially in the North Isles, it has probably decreased in recent years.

**SPANISH SPARROW** *Passer hispaniolensis* Very rare

There is 1 record, that of a male which was present on North Ronaldsay from 11th-19th August 1993.

**TREE SPARROW** *Passer montanus* An irregular passage visitor usually rare but occasionally uncommon. Very rare resident and formerly a rare breeding species

A small colony of approximately 10 pairs bred on Eday from 1961-1974. A pair also bred on Papa Westray in 1972. A female bird, first seen on North Ronaldsay in May 1994, paired with a male House Sparrow in 1997. Later that year at least 5 hybrids were seen. Successful interspecific breeding also took place in 1999. A hybrid was still present on the island in 2004.

Away from North Ronaldsay there have been occasional sightings of single birds from January to March. Spring passage has been recorded between 11th May and 29th June and in the autumn from 30th August to 3rd November, most recent sightings have been of 1-9 birds.

## FINCHES : Fringillidae

**CHAFFINCH** *Fringilla coelebs* Uncommon breeding resident; fairly common on passage

Small numbers of breeding pairs are found regularly in woods and gardens on Hoy, Mainland, Rousay and Shapinsay. Singing males have also been reported from Eday, Flotta and South Ronaldsay. The main passage movements in spring are from March to May and in autumn from late September and throughout October. Flocks of up to 60 birds may be recorded in winter.

**BRAMBLING** *Fringilla montifringilla* Fairly common but occasionally common passage visitor, uncommon in winter. Very rare breeding species

There have been a number of reports of singing males during May and June, but the only confirmed breeding record is of a single pair in 1988. The main spring passage movements are in April and May, but it is usually more numerous in autumn from mid-September through to mid-November. Small numbers may be present in winter, a flock of 200 in January 2004 is the largest so far recorded.

Photo ©Chris Booth

## GREENFINCH *Carduelis chloris*

Has increased since the mid-1970's and is now an uncommon resident breeding species and fairly common passage visitor

Breeding pairs have been reported from Burray, Eday, Mainland, Rousay, Shapinsay and South Ronaldsay, with a concentration in the Finstown, Kirkwall, St Ola and Stromness areas. The main passage movements are in April and October.

In recent years flocks of up to 70 birds have been recorded from November to February and smaller flocks of up to 20 birds regularly noted coming to bird tables to feed during the winter months. Even larger numbers have been attracted to Winter Farmland Bird Plots, with over 250 counted at a site in Firth.

## GOLDFINCH *Carduelis carduelis*

Formerly a rare visitor in winter, spring and autumn but in most recent years uncommon

Recorded rather irregularly from January to March, with sightings of 1-7 birds. The main spring passage is in late April and in May. There are records in June, July, August and September, but the majority of autumn reports are between 1st October and 29th December.

Photo ©Chris Booth

## SISKIN *Carduelis spinus*

Fairly common passage visitor, more numerous in autumn; very rare breeding species

The only confirmed breeding reports have been from Hoy and Rendall, but breeding has been suspected in Finstown and Rousay. Birds are occasionally recorded from January to early March with main spring passage from mid-March to June. In some years there are influxes in late June, July and into August, with autumn records from 9th September and main movements in late September and in October which can involve hundreds of birds. Numbers decline in November with few December records.

## LINNET (Lintie) *Carduelis cannabina*

Fairly common breeding resident and passage visitor

A widely distributed breeding species, especially where there are bushes. It has recently increased on North Ronaldsay. Formerly only small numbers were reported from December to February but now larger numbers appear to be overwintering.

There is a noticeable increase from mid-March and in April, while in autumn flocks build up in August through to October.

## TWITE (Heather lintie) *Carduelis flavirostris*

Fairly common but probably decreasing breeding resident, occasionally locally common in autumn

Widely distributed as a breeding species in small numbers throughout the islands. Flocks start building up in August and may reach several hundreds locally from October to March where there is suitable feeding.

## LESSER REDPOLL *Carduelis cabaret*

Very rare breeding species; uncommon passage migrant, has overwintered

The only confirmed breeding reports were in 1998, 1999 and 2004. In spring, recorded from 28th March with main passage in May and continuing into June and July. In autumn it is recorded from 1st September with highest numbers in October and into November. There are a few December records.

**COMMON REDPOLL** *Carduelis flammea* Fairly common passage migrant, more numerous in autumn; uncommon in winter and very rare breeding species

Apart from the records of Lesser Redpoll given above, breeding of Redpoll sp. has been suspected on a number of occasions, but has only been confirmed in 5 years with 1 pair being identified as belonging to the race *C.f.flammea.*

Irregular in winter with only small numbers reported. Spring passage is in April and May with a few records from June to August. The main autumn passage is in October, occasionally continuing into November and December. Most reports are of birds of the race *C.f.flammea* (Mealy Redpoll) but *C.f rostrata* (Greenland Redpoll) occurs fairly regularly in small numbers and very occasionally there are reports of *C.f.islandica.*

**ARCTIC REDPOLL** *Carduelis hornemanni* Usually a rare autumn visitor but uncommon in 1995, very rare in winter and spring

There are 3 records, all of single birds, between 16th February and 28th April. In autumn it has been recorded between 30th September and 17th December and, apart from 1995, the majority of sightings have been in October. In 1995 a minimum of 40 individuals was recorded between 7th November and 17th December.

**TWO-BARRED CROSSBILL** *Loxia leucoptera* Very rare visitor

There are 7 records, all occurring between 13th June and 27th August. 5 reports were of single birds, 1 of 2 birds and in 1990, 2-4 were seen in Evie between 18th and 21st August.

Photo - P & V Reynolds

**CROSSBILL** *Loxia curvirostra* An irruptive and irregular passage visitor which can range from rare to common

There have been occasional reports of birds in song, also alarming, on Hoy but, as yet, there has been no confirmation of breeding. There are sporadic records of small numbers, mainly 1-4 birds from January to May. Irruptions occur from late May continuing through to August with birds often being widespread throughout the islands. Numbers then quickly decline and there are only 2 December records.

Photo - Stuart Williams

**PARROT CROSSBILL** *Loxia pytyopsittacus* Very rare visitor

There are only 3 confirmed records, all of single birds : 29th October 1982 on Hoy, 2nd October 1983 on North Ronaldsay and 27th October 1985 in Holm.

**TRUMPETER FINCH** *Bucanetes githagineus* Very rare visitor

There is just 1 record, that of a bird present on Sanday from 25th-29th May 1981.

**COMMON ROSEFINCH** *Carpodacus erythrinus* Uncommon passage visitor in both spring and autumn

Spring records have occurred between 15th May and 30th June, with most sightings in the latter half of May. Singing males have been reported on a number of occasions, but there has been no evidence of breeding. There are 3 July records. Extreme dates in autumn are 4th August and 23rd November with the main passage in September.

Photo ©Stuart Williams

**BULLFINCH** *Pyrrhula pyrrhula* A passage visitor in varying numbers ranging from rare to fairly common, usually more numerous in autumn. Following large influxes in autumn, birds may remain throughout the winter and into spring

Small influxes have occurred in February, but the main spring passage is in April with the latest date on May 10th. There are records of single birds in June, July and August. Earliest date for autumn is 2nd October with most reports after mid-October. Many birds have been identified as belonging to the Northern race *P.p.pyrrhula.*

Photo ©Rod Thorne

**HAWFINCH** *Coccothraustes coccothraustes*
A rare passage visitor in spring and autumn, very occasionally uncommon. Most numerous in spring and very rare in winter

Recorded in spring between 21st March and 30th June with majority of reports in April and May. Autumn sightings are from 27th August -18th November, with most records in October and early November. There are 5 records from December to February. Most sightings are of single birds, but there are 7 records of 2 birds, 1 of 3 and 1 of 4 birds.

## NEW WORLD WARBLERS : Parulidae

Photo ©Stuart Williams

**TENNESSEE WARBLER** *Vermivora peregrina*
Very rare visitor

The only record is of a bird in Holm from 5th-7th September 1982.

**YELLOW WARBLER** Dendroica petechia Very rare visitor

A 1st year bird was on North Ronaldsay on 24th August 1992 and is the only record of this North American warbler.

Photo ©Stuart Williams

**YELLOW-RUMPED WARBLER** *Dendroica coronata*
Very rare visitor

Single birds were seen on North Ronaldsay on 13th October 1995 and at Costa, Evie from 31st October to 2nd November 2003.

## BUNTINGS : Emberizidae

### WHITE-THROATED SPARROW *Zonotrichia albicollis*
Very rare visitor

There was 1 on North Ronaldsay from 23rd-27th May 1996, the only record.

### LAPLAND BUNTING *Calcarius lapponicus*
Uncommon passage migrant, most numerous in autumn, rare in winter

There are occasional records in January, February and early March. Spring passage has been recorded between 28th March and 2nd June, with most records from mid-April to mid-May. There is 1 July record. In autumn the earliest date is 5th August but the majority of sightings are in September and October and in some years birds are still present in December.

### SNOW BUNTING (Snowflake) *Plectrophenax nivalis*
Common passage and winter visitor although, on the whole, numbers lower than in the early 1970's

Photo: Rod Thorne

Many wintering birds have left by the end of March, with usually only small numbers recorded in April and May with 1st July the last date. There is 1 record on 7th August and the earliest September date is 5th but passage is not regularly recorded until after mid-September, with highest counts in October and November.

### PINE BUNTING *Emberiza leucocephalos*
Very rare passage visitor in spring and rare in autumn

All records are of single birds. There was 1 in spring on 17th June 1995 on North Ronaldsay, and 9 records in autumn between 7th August and 9th November, with 6 of these in the period 15th-29th October.

### YELLOWHAMMER (Yellow yarling) *Emberiza citrinella*
Usually a rare passage visitor but occasionally uncommon, most numerous in autumn. Rare in winter. Formerly bred

The Yellowhammer decreased as a breeding species during the 20th century with the last breeding record in 1975. In spring, recorded between 14th March and 31st May with most sightings in April. Autumn passage is noted from 10th September to 11th November, with main movements in October. Recently there have been several January records with up to 6 birds being present on a Winter Farmland Bird Plot and 5 there in November and December .

### CIRL BUNTING *Emberiza cirlus*
Very rare visitor

There are just 2 records : a 1st winter female on Stronsay on 21st October 1994 and an adult female on North Ronaldsay from mid-August to 20th October 2002.

## ORTOLAN BUNTING *Emberiza hortulana*

Usually a rare passage visitor but occasionally uncommon, slightly more numerous in autumn

In spring, recorded between 6th May and 19th June and in autumn between 18th August and 25th October, with most sightings in September.

## CRETZSCHMAR'S BUNTING *Emberiza caesia*

Very rare

A male seen at Rothiesholm Head, Stronsay on 4th and 5th May 1998 is the only record.

## YELLOW-BROWED BUNTING *Emberiza chrysophrys*

Very rare visitor

There are 2 records, both of single birds : 22nd and 23rd September 1992 on North Ronaldsay and 4th-5th May 1998 at Rackwick, Hoy.

## RUSTIC BUNTING *Emberiza rustica*

Rare passage visitor

Recorded in spring between 16th May and 26th June. In autumn between 18th September and 2nd November, all records are of single birds.

## LITTLE BUNTING *Emberiza pusilla*

Rare visitor in autumn, very rare in winter and in spring

The only record in spring is of 1 on 11th May 1986 in St Ola. Has been recorded regularly on autumn passage since 1984 with annual totals of between 1 and 7 birds, extreme dates 5th September and 19th November. 1 bird first seen on Stronsay 30th October 1993 was last seen there on 10th February 1994.

## YELLOW-BREASTED BUNTING *Emberiza aureola*

Very rare autumn visitor

There are 9 records, all of single birds, and extreme dates 4th September and 1st October.

Photo ©Chris Booth

## REED BUNTING *Emberiza schoeniclus*

Fairly common breeding resident and passage migrant

A widespread breeding species which increased in the middle part of the 20th century but has now decreased. Evidence of passage on North Ronaldsay in September and October.

Photo ©Stuart Williams

## BLACK-HEADED BUNTING *Emberiza melanocephala*

Very rare visitor

There are 10 records, all of single birds, between 17th June and 4th October.

## CORN BUNTING (Skitter broltie, Thistle cock) *Emberiza calandra*

Formerly a resident breeding species, now a very rare passage migrant

This species decreased as a breeding species during the 20th century and the last confirmed breeding record was on Stronsay in 1993. Former strongholds were on Sanday and Stronsay. Recent records have been of only 1-2 birds, the last was in 1999

## Category D species and escapes

The following are some of the species recorded in Orkney, that are either escaped birds or category D species in that there is reasonable doubt that they have occurred here in a wild state.

### FLAMINGO *Phoenicopteridae sp.*

A bird of the Chilean race was present in St Ola in January 1974 and was later found dead; 1, of unknown race, was seen in Westray on 19th June 1979.

### BLACK SWAN *Cygnus atratus*

A bird which arrived in South Ronaldsay in April 1995 was still present in Orkney, but on Loch of Harray, in 2004. In 2001 a pair bred near Kirkwall and reared 3 young. The male disappeared and 1 young died, the remaining 3 birds were last seen on the Peerie Sea in April 2002.

### BAR-HEADED GOOSE *Anser indicus*

There are 11 records of 1-2 birds 1969-2004, with most sightings in May and June.

### RED-BREASTED GOOSE *Branta ruficollis*

An adult, Mill Sand, Tankerness on 20th May 2004 and then at Eve's Howe, Deerness on 2nd June.

### FALCATED DUCK *Anas falcata*

A male was shot on Shapinsay 24th November 2000.

### BOOTED EAGLE *Hieraaetus pennatus*

A pale phase bird was seen on North Ronaldsay on 22nd June 2000.

### SAKER FALCON *Falco cherrug*

There have been several sightings of this species which probably refer to escaped birds, including reports in 1983 and 1999

### DEMOISELLE CRANE *Anthropoides virgo*

There were 2 in Deerness on 14th May 1863.

### EURASIAN EAGLE OWL *Bubo bubo*

1 was shot on Sanday in 1830.

### BLUE ROCK THRUSH *Monticola solitarius*

A bird of this species was present on North Ronaldsay from 29th August to 6th September 1966.

### PALLAS'S ROSEFINCH *Carpodacus roseus*

A 1st year bird was on North Ronaldsay from 2nd June to 14th July 1988.

### RED-HEADED BUNTING *Emberiza bruniceps*

There have been 11 recorded sightings of male birds in the period 1931-1989, with extreme dates 10th May and 11th August.

### LAZULI BUNTING *Passerina amoena*

A male was present in Holm from 31st May 1964 for about 1 week.

Bearded seal, Kirkwall, 1988 ©P & V Reynolds

Geologists appear to be of the opinion that, following the last ice age, a land bridge between Orkney and Scotland would not have persisted for long enough in conditions suitable for animals to be able pass over it. This would suggest that land mammals, except perhaps the otter and bats, are either deliberate introductions or have arrived accidentally. There is one species, the Orkney vole, that is unique to Orkney. Research is taking place at present to find the origins of this vole, as well as those of other small mammals such as pygmy shrew and mice.

Orkney Vole ©P Et V Reynolds

Marine mammals, on the other hand, are well represented. There are large populations of common and grey seals, while the offshore waters provide suitable feeding grounds for whales and dolphins.

The list follows the sequence and scientific nomenclature of the Handbook of British Mammals (3rd edition) edited by Gordon G Corbet and Stephen Harris.

Risso's Dolphins, Holm, May 2005 ©Drew Kennedy

Marwick towards Hoy ©Drew Kennedy

## INSECTIVORES : Order Insectivora

### HEDGEHOGS : Erinaceidae

**HEDGEHOG** *Erinaceus europaeus* — Common

Occurs throughout the mainland of Britain and Ireland; has also been introduced into a number of smaller islands.

Easily recognisable, the back and top of the head are covered with sharp pointed spines, the rest of the body with coarse hair; specimens with light coloured spines are occasionally reported. It is mainly nocturnal.

The hedgehog is a fairly recent addition to Orkney's fauna. The first introduction took place in about 1870 but this almost certainly failed. The next attempts were made in the 1930's and 1940's and by 1950 it was probably established in the East Mainland, Shapinsay, Westray and possibly Hoy, and appeared to have reached the West Mainland by 1960. Other introductions were to Egilsay (1950's), Wyre (1960's), again to Hoy (1960's), North Ronaldsay, Eday and Sanday (1970's), Stronsay (1980), Rousay and again Wyre in the 1980's. Hedgehogs are also present on Burray, Flotta, Graemsay and South Ronaldsay but details of when they were introduced are not known.

The introduction of the hedgehog was not a sensible one and the effects on the ecology of the different islands are difficult to assess. Although the main food is invertebrates taken on the ground, they will prey on the eggs and young of ground nesting birds. It has also been suggested that they may be responsible for the drastic decline in the toad population.

On North Ronaldsay, in the 1980's, in an attempt to improve the breeding success of ground nesting birds, over 200 animals were live trapped and moved to the Scottish mainland.

Hedgehogs begin hibernating in late October, but there are reports of them being seen, especially in mild weather, throughout the winter. The main emergence from hibernation is from the second week of April, and this is often indicated by the presence of corpses on the road. Juveniles have been seen from the first week of July.

### SHREWS : Soricidae

**PYGMY SHREW** *Sorex minutus* — Fairly common
**(Nebbit mouse, Roan mouse, Sheer mouse)**

Found throughout mainland Britain and on many small islands.

The smallest land mammal in Orkney with a weight of just 3-4gms. It has a body length of about 50mm, including the long pointed nose, and with the long tail, a total length of 90mm. The colour is medium brown above and dirty white on the underside. The pygmy shrew is active both during the day and at night, feeding mainly on invertebrates including woodlice and spiders.

How this mammal arrived in Orkney is uncertain. It could possibly have crossed from mainland Scotland on a glacial bridge or have been transported amongst animal fodder by early human settlers. Some insight into the origin of the pygmy shrew may be obtained from the current DNA research.

Very little is known about its earlier status, although Baikie and Heddle thought that it was not very common. It has recently been recorded from the following islands : Burray, Copinsay, Flotta, Graemsay, Holm of Grimbister, Hoy, Mainland, Rousay, Shapinsay, South Ronaldsay,

Stronsay and Westray. Although fairly common on some of the islands, loss of habitat could be responsible for its decline on others.

It is widely distributed, particularly in moorland and rough grassland, and can be found from sea level to at least 300m (Hoy). In late autumn and winter it may take shelter in houses.

### WATER SHREW *Neomys fodiens* — Status uncertain, reported only from Hoy

Found over much of mainland Britain but rather local in northern Scotland.

Similar in form to the pygmy shrew but much larger, with a length of approximately 130mm and a weight of 12gms. The upper body fur is black in colour and the underside silvery grey. It is most active at night.

The present status of this species in Orkney is unknown, the only possible reports have come from Hoy. A water shrew was stated, by Baikie and Heddle, to have been killed near Melsetter in 1847. More recently there are 2 published records of sightings in the Braebuster burn, in August 1959 and on 13th May 1964. As yet no specimens have been critically examined.

## BATS : Order Chiroptera

Bats have always been considered to be rare in Orkney but 5 different species have been recorded and there is 1 known colony of common pipistrelles. In most years there are 1 or 2 sightings from widespread localities.

## VESPERTILIONID BATS : Vespertilionidae

### NOCTULE *Nyctalus noctula* — Very rare

In Britain the noctule is confined to England, Wales and southwest Scotland.

A large migratory bat, the fur on the upper parts is golden brown in colour becoming duller and lighter brown underneath. The wings are long and narrow with a span of 32-40cm.

There are 3 records :

- 1976 14th Jun A pregnant female on North Ronaldsay
- 1978 29th Sep A young female, Sanday
- 1988 25th Oct 1 found alive, South Ronaldsay was sent to Aberdeen for release

### COMMON PIPISTRELLE *Pipistrellus pipistrellus* — Rare, locally uncommon

Widely distributed throughout Britain and Ireland. Calls at 45kHz.

Photo ©Chris Booth

Together with the soprano pipistrelle, this is the smallest and commonest British bat, with a wingspan of 18-24cm. The fur is rufous to dark brown above and greyer underneath.

There is a small colony of common pipistrelles in Hoy. This was discovered in 1994, when a minimum of 5 individuals was seen. Bats, almost certainly of this species, were seen regularly for many years during the summer in Stromness. The probable roost was in the old Academy but there have been no sightings in Stromness since 1991, following renovations to this building.

There have been 4 common pipistrelles found in the Kirkwall area that have been examined in the hand. These include a female, injured when caught by a cat on 29th June 1995. It gave birth a few days later but, unfortunately, both mother and baby died.

Since 2000 there have been sightings of 1-2 bats, during July and August in Finstown. These bats have been calling at 45 kHz and are thought to be common pipistrelles. In 2004 at least 3 were seen together at one time and it seems probable that a summer roost has been established in this area.

## NATHUSIUS' PIPISTRELLE *Pipistrellus nathusii* Very rare

A migratory species whose status in Britain is uncertain, although colonies have been found in England and Northern Ireland.

A small bat, slightly larger than the common pipistrelle, with a wingspan of 22-25cm. Nathusius' pipistrelle also has a different dentition with a large first pre-molar visible on the outside of the dental arch. In summer the fur is red to chestnut-brown but, following moult in August, is darker brown with grey tips which give it a frosted appearance.

There are 2 records :

- 1995 12th Jun 1 found alive in South Ronaldsay died the following day
- 2002 7th Jun 1 found dead on North Ronaldsay

## BROWN LONG-EARED BAT *Plecotus auritus* Very rare

Widespread throughout mainland Britain and Ireland.

A distinguishing feature is its very long ears, which are obvious in flight. The fur is brown to buff in colour, the wings are broad with a span of 24-28.5cm.

There are the following records :

- 1931 18th Feb 1 found alive in a store at the lighthouse at Start Point, Sanday
- 1948 11th Oct 1 caught alive at Roseness, Holm
- 1987 Between 18th and 25th Aug 1 was seen flying at Banks Farm, West Mainland

## HOARY BAT *Lasiurus cinereus* Very rare

A North American bat capable of undertaking long distance migratory flights.

A large bat, the fur is yellowish brown to mahogony brown in colour, the hairs are tipped with white giving a frosted or hoary appearance.

A specimen of this species was found in September 1847 on South Ronaldsay.

## BAT sp

Apart from the sightings already mentioned, it has been possible to collect a number of reports of bats, none of which were specifically identified, for 1960 and from 1976-2004. The records come from many different parts of the islands and are most frequent from July to October.

Monthly distribution of sightings - 1960 and 1976-2004

| J | F | M | A | M | J | J | A | S | O | N | D |
|---|---|---|---|---|---|---|---|---|---|---|---|
| 1 | 0 | 1 | 2 | 3 | 4 | 14 | 13 | 10 | 15 | 6 | 0 |

Some of the bats were described as small and of pipistrelle type and others larger, so it would appear that more than 1 species was involved. The majority of sightings have been of single bats, but 2 have been seen on 4 occasions and on 2 occasions 3 bats were seen. Exceptional was the presence of 12 at the Bu, Hoy on 2nd June 1998.

# LAGOMORPHS : Order Lagomorpha

## RABBITS AND HARES : Leporidae

### RABBIT (Cuning) *Oryctolagus cuniculus*

Very common

Widespread in mainland Britain up to the tree line and on many small islands.

Photo ©Chris Booth

Upper parts are greyish-brown in colour and the undersides white. It has a white tail with brown above. A length of up to 40cm and a weight of 1.2-2.0kg.

The rabbit was introduced into Britain by the Normans and appears to have been firmly established in Orkney by the 17th century. Low, at the end of the 18th century, noted that many of the islands swarmed with rabbits. At this time, and in the early 19th century, large numbers of skins were exported. There may then have been a decline in the population as Buckley and Harvie-Brown in 1891 commented that nowhere, apart from Eynhallow, were there large numbers.

In the early 1950's rabbits were common until the arrival in 1954 of myxamatosis, which spread throughout the islands, reducing the rabbit population to about 10% of its previous numbers. Although the population subsequently recovered, on some islands such as Auskerry, the Green Holms and Eynhallow, they were completely wiped out.

Although it favours areas of sandy soil such as many of the areas of sandy links, it can be found from the seashore to the tops of the highest hills and has even been seen on the summit of Ward Hill, Hoy. At present there are records from Burray, Copinsay, Eday, Egilsay, Flotta, Gairsay, Glimps Holm, Graemsay, Hoy, Lamb Holm, Mainland, North Ronaldsay, Papa Westray, Rousay, Sanday, Shapinsay, South Fara, South Ronaldsay, Stronsay, Westray and Wyre.

Colour variations are not uncommon, including black and sandy coloured, also some have been seen with white markings.

### BROWN HARE *Lepus europeaus*

Confined to Mainland, where common and widely distributed

On mainland Britain it occurs in open farmland areas, especially where cereal crops are grown.

Photo ©Leonard Bain

Distinguished from the rabbit by its larger size and longer ears with black tips. The upper parts are reddish brown, the belly white and the tail white with black on the upper side. Length 54cm weight 3-3.5kg. It does not change colour in winter.

The brown hare was introduced in 1832 and by 1891 it was noted that it occurred on Eday, Hoy, Mainland, Rousay, Shapinsay and South Ronaldsay. Since that time it has become extinct on all islands apart from Mainland and possibly Rousay but there is no information on when these extinctions occurred. On Rousay it was thought that the last hare was killed in 1977 but there was a possible sighting in 1998.

On Mainland it was common in the 1950's and 1960's following the reduction of the rabbit population by myxamatosis. There is mention in The Orcadian newspaper, dated 15th

December 1955, of the recent export to Germany of 3 tons of hares that had been obtained locally. Numbers seemed to have fluctuated and there appeared to be a decline between 1970 and the mid-1990's. Since then they have increased and are widely distributed throughout Mainland.

Brown hares are probably commonest in rough grassland and moorland around the coast, but can be seen on the seashore and also the high moorland hills. They are most obvious in spring when groups gather in fields and there is little growth of vegetation to conceal them. Leverets have been found as early as 24th February.

## MOUNTAIN HARE *Lepus timidus*

Confined to Hoy where it is fairly common

Photo ©Chris Booth

Native to the Highlands of Scotland, it has been introduced into other areas of Britain including some of the larger islands.

Smaller in size than the brown hare, with a length of 50cm and weighing 2.8kg. It has comparatively shorter ears with only small black tips. In summer the coat is dusky brown and mainly white in winter. There is no black on top of the tail. Unlike the brown hare, which runs away when disturbed, the mountain hare will, at times, take refuge in burrows.

Mountain hares appear to have been present on Hoy at the beginning of the 16th century as there is a reference by John Bellenden, in 1529, of white hares being hunted there by dogs. They were probably extinct by the end of the 17th century and this is certainly true for the 19th century, as it was confirmed by both Baikie and Heddle and Buckley and Harvie-Brown. A re-introduction took place some time between 1898 and 1910 and they are now fairly common in the north end of Hoy. Mountain hares occur mainly at heights above 100m, but can occasionally be seen at sea level.

The coat change from brown to white takes place from October to January and reverts to brown from February to late April, but a few may still show some white in early June. Young hares, just over half grown, have been seen from the first week of June.

# RODENTS : Order Rodentia

## VOLES : Arvicolinae

## ORKNEY VOLE *Microtus arvalis orcadensis*

Locally abundant

(**Cuttick, Cuttoo** - E Mainland; **Levellyn, Vole mouse, Volo** - Evie; **Voloo** - Harray)

Photo ©P & V Reynoldss

A subspecies of the common vole *Microtus arvalis*, which is widespread in Continental Europe. The only other part of Britain where the common vole is found is on the Channel Island of Guernsey. It is larger than either the bank and field voles, which are found in the rest of Britain, and has a distinctive dentition.

This vole is unique to Orkney. It has a stocky body, small rounded ears, a blunt head and a tail which is about one-third the length of the body. The fur on the upper parts of the body is dark brown while the underside is lighter, although colour variations, including black, do occur. The head and body length average about 120mm and large specimens can weigh up to 90gm.

Writers in the 19th century believed this vole to be the field vole *Microtus agrestis* and it was not until 1904 that Millais suggested that it was a different species. Recent research suggests that its origins are in south-western Europe, specifically France and northern Spain. It was probably introduced into Orkney by Neolithic settlers in about 3,500BC.

It is present on the islands of Burray, Hunda, Mainland, Rousay, Sanday, South Ronaldsay, Westray and has recently become established on Eday, where an introduction of voles from Westray was made in 1987 and 1988.

The Orkney vole occurs in a wide variety of semi-natural habitats from sea level to the summits of moorland hills, and in maximum densities in rough grassland, including along ditches and fence lines. The runs, or "highways", of the voles are a common sight, particularly in winter when the vegetation has died down. On Mainland, agricultural crops seem to be avoided although this type of habitat is used on Eday.

The loss of the semi-natural habitats has probably resulted in a recent reduction in numbers. It is an important prey item for short-eared owls, kestrels and hen harriers but the main predator of the Orkney vole is the cat, both domestic and feral.

## RATS AND MICE : Murinae

### WOOD MOUSE or Long tailed field mouse *Apodemus sylvaticus* Fairly common
**(Bank mouse** - North Ronaldsay)

Widespread on mainland Britain apart from some open mountainous areas. Present also on many islands.

Photo ©Gil Steven

An attractive animal, with dark brown upper parts, white underparts, large ears and a long tail. Has a body length of 93mm, with a weight of 19gms. Very active, it climbs well and often bounds.

The wood mouse was probably introduced into Orkney by early human settlers in fodder for domestic animals. In the 18th and 19th centuries it was considered to be fairly common in fields and stack yards. This species appears to have a limited distribution but it is possibly under-recorded, being mainly nocturnal. Since 1972 it has been recorded on Copinsay, Eday, Graemsay, Hoy, Linga Holm, Mainland, North Ronaldsay, Papa Westray, Sanday, Shapinsay, South Ronaldsay and Stronsay.

It is widespread and fairly common on Mainland, particularly in cereal fields and rough grassland, but less common in heather moorland. There may have been a decline in the population due to changes in farming practice, especially with fewer stacks being kept in fields throughout the winter.

Following the harvest in the autumn some wood mice may seek shelter in houses and other buildings. It has been recorded feeding from bird tables and amongst garden crops.

### HOUSE MOUSE *Mus domesticus* Common

Widespread on mainland Britain and most inhabited small islands.

The body is dull greyish-brown on the upper parts and slightly lighter underneath. The ears are small compared to those of the wood mouse and the tail comparatively shorter. Average head and body length 75mm and weight 18gms.

It is not known when the house mouse first arrived in Orkney but it appears to have been common in the 18th and 19th centuries, wherever there was human habitation. It was also said to be very common in corn stacks and many were killed during threshing. There is little information about its present status but it is widely distributed throughout the islands and appears to remain common around farms and farm buildings. The present lack of corn stacks may have resulted in a decline in the population in some areas.

Since 1965 there are records from Burray, Copinsay, Eday, Egilsay, Flotta, Graemsay, Holm of Grimbister, Hoy, Mainland, North Fara, North Ronaldsay, Papa Westray, Rousay, Sanday, Shapinsay, Stronsay, South Ronaldsay, Swona, Westray and Wyre.

## COMMON RAT or Brown Rat *Rattus norvegicus* — Very common

Found in urban areas throughout the world and, in Britain, in all but the most exposed mountain areas and a few offshore islands.

The fur of the upperparts is usually grey brown in colour and underneath it is pale grey. It has a body length up to 280mm, with the tail length slightly less. Weight up to 500gms. The ears are small and finely furred and the tail usually dark brown above and light below. Very active and swims well. Has an onmivorous diet, eating both vegetable and animal matter.

The common rat probably reached Britain in the first half of the 18th century and was thought to be introduced into Orkney from ships. It was well established on Mainland Orkney at the end of the 18th century. According to historical writers, there were population fluctuations during the 19th century. It was established on Stronsay by 1868 and Sanday and South Ronaldsay by 1888.

This species is now very common and well distributed, being found on all the larger islands except, probably, North Ronaldsay and Westray. On Papa Westray it was common in the 1980's but then declined and the last records are in the early 1990's; it is now thought to be extinct on the island. It is absent also from Auskerry and Copinsay. Common rats appeared on Eynhallow between August 1997 and May 1998, the method of introduction is open to speculation. Following a pest control programme there have been no further signs of rats on the island.

On several occasions specimens with white markings have been reported from Dounby, Harray and Stromness.

## SHIP RAT or Black Rat *Rattus rattus* — **Probably extinct**

Occurs in urban areas throughout the tropics and sub-tropics. It now has a very restricted range in Britain.

Smaller than the common rat, the ship rat has a body length 240mm, the tail is longer than the body and uniformly dark in colour. Weight about 200gms. The fur can be black in colour but is often grey-black and paler underneath. Compared to the common rat, the ears of the ship rat are large and almost hairless. It climbs well but is less inclined to swim than the previous species. Has an omnivorous diet although it is more vegetarian than the common rat.

The ship rat is thought to have arrived in Britain during Roman times. According to Low in 1770 it had declined in Orkney during the 18th century, having been ousted by the common rat, and was then confined to South Ronaldsay. It was still present there in the 1930's as Groundwater gives 3 records, the last in 1938. There are also 2 possible records from Kirkwall in the 1940's.

In 1939 a German grain ship ran aground below Skaill in Westray and ship rats which were on board made their way ashore. They became established on the island for several decades and for a time were a pest on some of the farms. The last definite record there was in 1968 although it was thought to be still present until the early 1970's. It is now probably extinct on Westray.

## WHALES, DOLPHINS AND PORPOISES : Order Cetacea

A total of 19 species has been recorded in Orkney waters since 1929 and there is an historical reference to 1 other, the blue whale. This total is not as high as that of Shetland, which is due to the fact that Orkney lies rather too far east of the migration routes that usually follow the Continental Shelf.

Sightings are rather irregular but may occur at any time of the year, although the period from May to October is usually the most productive. Cetacean watching can be carried out from a boat or from the shore. For the former, the ferry crossings of the Pentland Firth and from Kirkwall to the North Isles provide excellent opportunities. Land based watching can be undertaken from a number of sites including the shores of Scapa Flow and vantage points such as those shown on the map on page 99.

Views of cetaceans are often very brief and this can make identification difficult. It is important to note size of the animal, colour and markings; height and shape of blow (if there is one ); position, size and shape of dorsal fin; head shape; also behaviour, before a conclusion is reached.

### BALEEN WHALES : Suborder Mysteceti

Balaenopteridae : Genus Megaptera

### HUMPBACK WHALE *Megaptera novaeangliae* Very rare

A migratory species with a worldwide distribution but rare in the north east Atlantic. Has been seen fairly regularly off Shetland in recent years.

A large bulky whale, 12-15m in length. The body, which is mainly black or grey in colour and lighter around the throat and belly, is often encrusted with barnacles. The flippers are long, frequently all white in colour, and the tail flukes are broad and scalloped on the rear margins. The underside of the tail may be partially white, with markings which make it possible to

Photo ©Chris Booth

identify individuals. The blow is bushy, about 3m in height. It frequently breaches and flipper slaps and, when diving, typically arches its back before raising its tail flukes out of the water.

The humpback whale is the most recent addition to the Orkney cetacean list. There have been 5 records of sightings :

- The first was of 3 seen in Echnaloch Bay, Burray on 27th February 2001. They were watched for about 45 minutes, the largest of the whales was estimated to be 10m in length.
- A single humpback was seen from a fishing boat about 4km southeast of Mull Head, Papa Westray in the last week of July 2003.
- 3 were observed on 12th November 2003 in Scapa Flow off Greenigoe, Orphir. They were seen to breach and 1 whale turned on its side with a flipper pointing up in the air. The whales stayed in the Scapa Flow area for several days, the last sighting of them was late in the afternoon of 17th November, between Hunda and the Nevi Skerry.
- On 13th August 2004 one spent some time around a dive boat west of Eynhallow. It was estimated to be between 7 and 10 metres in length and the tail fluke to be 2m across.
- On 4th July 2005 1 was seen from MV Hascosay off the east side of Orkney

Stranding : The only recorded stranding is of a badly decomposed whale found near the Broch of Gurness, Evie on 27th February 2004. The length was estimated to be 10 metres.

## RORQUALS : Genus Balaenoptera

### FIN WHALE or Common Rorqual (Finner) *Balaenoptera physalus* — Very rare

Worldwide distribution, but commoner in the southern hemisphere.

The second largest whale, it may reach a length of 26m. Dark grey above, white underneath with a small, backward sloping, dorsal fin situated towards the posterior third. The right side of the head is white around the mouth cavity but grey on the left side. The blow is a tall narrow column up to 6m in height.

The fin whale, although now very rare in Orkney, was apparently much commoner in the 19th century. Buckley and Harvie-Brown mention strandings of specimens of 21-24m in length. It was sometimes seen in Scapa Flow, 3 being present there throughout one summer. One, which measured 18.8m, was stranded on Hunda in 1852 and another, which stranded in December 1884, contained a foetus 2.1m in length.

There are only 3 definite 20th century records :

- 1923 25th June 1 West Mainland. Unfortunately no other details are available
- 1982 12th Sept 1 was hit by a fishing boat off Westray and stranded alive on Papa Westray on 13th September. It subsequently died. Length 13.7m
- 1985 2nd July 1 was seen between North Ronaldsay and Fair Isle. It surfaced twice and then breached

A sighting of 1 off Hoy on 30th July 1998 is given in the Sea Watch Foundation publication *Soundings*. Unfortunately it has not been possible to obtain any further information to confirm this record.

### BLUE WHALE *Balaenoptera musculus* — Very rare

Worldwide distribution but only occurs in small numbers in the north Atlantic.

This is the largest whale, length often 24-28m. The body colour is bluish-grey with extensive mottling, the underside may have a yellowish colouration. The dorsal fin is small and situated at least two thirds along the body. The whale may show its tail flukes when diving and the blow is vertical and slender, up to 9m in height.

Historical reports are rather vague and there are no confirmed records of this species in Orkney waters. Buckley and Harvie-Brown mention that a probable Sibbald's rorqual, which could refer to a blue whale, was stranded at Longhope either in 1883 or 1884. It was over 15m in length.

## SEI WHALE *Balaenoptera borealis*

Very rare

Worldwide distribution, mainly found in polar and temperate seas.

Length 12-16m with a dark grey body and greyish-white throat. The dorsal fin, which is relatively tall and sickle shaped, is situated nearly two thirds along the back. The blow is vertical, about 3m in height, and is seen simultaneously with the dorsal fin before the whale rolls below the surface.

The only record is of 1, 14.7m in length, that stranded on Papa Westray on 3rd October 1929.

## MINKE WHALE or Lesser Rorqual *Balaenoptera acutorostrata*

Common, probably present throughout the year but most often recorded May to October

Worldwide distribution.

The minke whale is the smallest and commonest of the rorqual whales, with a length of 7-9m. The body is dark grey to black with white underside and the flipper has a white diagonal band.

The dorsal fin is sickle shaped, relatively tall and situated two-thirds along the back. The blow is rarely visible, the usual view is of a rolling back and dorsal fin but, when lunge-feeding, the head may come right out of the water. Often breaches.

Historically, Buckley and Harvie-Brown quoted a correspondent who noted that this species appeared "not infrequently" in Scapa Flow. They also gave details of a dead female, found stranded at the end of 1884, which contained a foetus 1.8m in length.

The minke whale is probably present in Orkney waters throughout the year. There are sightings in all months apart from February and March, although there is a stranding of a live whale in February. The finding of a freshly dead calf measuring 2.27m in December would suggest that

Minke whale breaching off Horse of Copinsay - Photo ©Colin Thomson

the females give birth close to the islands. Most commonly seen from June to October, there is an obvious peak in August. The majority of records are of single whales but at least 2 have been seen together on 6 occasions and there are 2 records of 4-5.

Minke whales are quite often seen in the vicinity of headlands and may stay in an area for several weeks if there are shoals of fish present. One, watched from the MV Pentland Venture in the Pentland Firth, was seen to breach 74 times in succession.

Apart from the calf already mentioned there have been 24 individual strandings in the period 1978-2004. Of these strandings, 16 occurred between June and October and 5 of the whales were still alive when they came ashore. Of these live whales 2 were apparently successfully rescued, as they were moved back into the water and swam away. 2 others had injuries, 1 had probably been hit by a boat and 1 was entangled in netting, both subsequently died. The strandings involved both adult and immature whales, 16 of the stranded animals were measured, 10 were between 4.5m and 5.8m in length and 6 were between 6m and 8.7m. It was possible to determine the sex of 12 of these whales, 9 were males and 3 were females.

## TOOTHED WHALES : Suborder Odontoceti

### SPERM WHALES : Physeteridae

**SPERM WHALE** *Physeter macrocephalus* — Uncommon; rare prior to 1975

Worldwide distribution. Found mainly in the deep water of temperate, tropical and sub-polar seas of both northern and southern hemispheres.

Photo - Sperm whales in Scapa Flow ©Chris Booth

Photo ©Chris Booth

Length 11-18m with a robust body and very large head. There is no dorsal fin but a hump about two-thirds along the body. The skin, which is dark brown or grey in colour, has a wrinkled or shrivelled appearance. The blowhole is located on the left hand side of the head and the blow is bushy and angled forwards. When diving, the whale raises it tail flukes in the air. Males only have visible teeth, and these, which are situated in the lower jaw, are 36-50 in number.

The frequency with which this species has occurred seems to have fluctuated in the last 300 years. Low, writing in the 18th century, stated that it was often driven ashore. There must then have been a change in the 19th century as Buckley and Harvie-Brown suggested that their informants considered it to be rare. This was still the case for most of the 20th century with only 2 records up until 1975. The first, that of a new-born calf stranded in September 1916, must be considered to be very doubtful, as most sperm whale births take place in equatorial waters. There is now no way of verifying this record. The other record was of a sighting off Rousay in August 1936.

Since 1975 there have been a number of sightings and strandings. As far as is known, only males have occurred, the females rarely move north into the colder waters of the north-eastern Atlantic.

Sightings, 1975-2004 :

- 1976 Oct 6 or 7 seen in Scapa Flow on several occasions during 1 day from an Islander aircraft. It is probable that they were immature males of varying ages.
- 1981 22nd Sept 1 Scapa Flow, c18m in length, seen from an Islander aircraft
- 1993 22nd Feb 6 Scapa Flow present until 25th Mar. 4 of these whales were about 15m in length, the other 2 slightly smaller. Because of the lack of food and the very strong possibility that they would strand, it was decided to mount an operation to move them out of the Flow. On 25th Mar. a flotilla of boats succeeded in shepherding the whales south through Hoxa Sound, and they were last seen heading out into the Pentland Firth.
- 1998 14th Apr 7 present until at least 21st April, thought to be between 11m and 15m in length. It was difficut to follow their movements because of bad weather. An aerial survey failed to find them on the 24th April.
- 1998 29th May 1 seen blowing off Swona.
- 2002 27th-28th Nov A minimum of 10 (although some observers reported 13), present in Holm Sound. Some individuals were thought to have been 15m in length.

Strandings, 1975-2004 :

- There have been 15 stranding incidents and all whales examined have been males. In only 2 cases have live animals been involved. The other 13 have all been of single animals, some of which had been dead for some time and had probably drifted a considerable distance before coming ashore. The lengths have ranged from 9.9-18.7m with 10 being in the range 12-15m.

Both live strandings have occurred at Backaskaill, Sanday

- 1984 13th Dec 1 length 16.8m

Mass stranding on Sanday - Photo ©Rod Thorne

- 1994 7th Dec A mass stranding involving 11 whales, ranging from 12.29-13.39m in length. One of the whales had its lower jaw missing but the wound appeared to have healed satisfactorily. It was not possible to rescue any of these whales.

## Monodontidae

### WHITE WHALE or Beluga *Delphinapterus leucas* Very rare

Distribution restricted to Arctic and sub-Arctic seas of the northern hemisphere.

Adults are white in colour with a dorsal ridge instead of a fin and paddle-shaped flippers. It has a small rounded head and short beak. Length 3-5m.

There are just 4 records - 2 sightings and 2 strandings.

Sightings :

- 1960 Oct 1 Holm Sound
- 1964 Aug 1 was present on the Scapa Flow side of the 4th barrier for 2 days. It was estimated to be 4.6m in length

Strandings :

- 1845 Oct 1 Auskerry, following an easterly gale
- 1981 Oct 1 Marwick, Sandwick, Mainland - badly decomposed. Length c3.6m

### NARWHAL *Monodon monocerus* Very rare

Found mainly in the deep waters of the high Arctic.

The body is stout and mottled grey-green in colour. It has a bulbous head with only a slight beak, there is no dorsal fin. Length 4-5m. Adult males have a long tusk.

- There is just 1 record, that of 2 seen off Gairsay in late June 1949.

BEAKED WHALES : Ziphiidae

## NORTHERN BOTTLENOSE WHALE *Hyperoodon ampullatus* Very rare

A deep water species found in the North Atlantic. Occurs off the Continental Shelf to the north and west of Scotland and around the Faroe Islands, also in deep canyons in the southern Bay of Biscay.

Length 7-9m with a bulbous forehead, a small dolphin-like beak, and a triangular or slightly curved dorsal fin situated two-thirds along the back. Its colour varies from dark grey to brown, becoming paler with age. Has a bushy blow up to 2m in height. Males have 2, occasionally 4 teeth at the tip of the lower jaw.

This may have been the beaked whale mentioned by Buckley and Harvie-Brown who thought it was common at times around the coasts. The only confirmed 19th century record was of 1 obtained in 1845. This is the type specimen of this species under the Latin names of *Hyperoodon latifrons* and *Lagenocetus latifrons*. The skull, lower jaw, some vertebrae, ribs and flippers are in the Natural History Museum, London.

There have been 3 more recent strandings of single whales, all of which have probably drifted for some time and distance before reaching Orkney.

- 1995 24th Jun Adult male, Auskerry, length 9.44m, the stomach contained many squid beaks
- 2001 Apr North side of Quoy Ness, Sanday. It was not measured and from photographs of the skull was thought to be an immature male
- 2001 9th Nov Adult female, 7.5m in length, Bay of Skaill, Sandwick, Mainland. The whale had probably been dead for about a month and the body was emaciated. The skeleton is in the National Museum of Scotland, Edinburgh

## CUVIER'S BEAKED WHALE *Ziphius cavirostris* Very rare

Thought to have a worldwide distribution in temperate and tropical waters. Found mainly in deep offshore water.

Has a long, robust body with a small curved dorsal fin about two-thirds along the back. The colour is variable ranging from orange-brown to greyish but the head can be almost white. The shape of the head is unusual, with a sloping forehead and distinct beak, the lower jaw protruding slightly. Males have 2 teeth at the tip of the lower jaw.

There have been 3 strandings of this beaked whale :

- 1920 2nd Oct 1, East Mainland, 7.3m in length
- 1963 Early Jan 1, Rackwick, Hoy, c6m in length
- 1963 12th Sept 1, Rackwick, Hoy, female

## SOWERBY'S BEAKED WHALE *Mesoplodon bidens* Very rare

Apparently found only in the northern North Atlantic.

About 5m long with a slim body and a relatively long slender beak. The small curved dorsal fin is situated about two-thirds along the body, the flippers are small and the tail flukes have a concave trailing edge. Males have single teeth situated midway along the lower jaw. Colour dark grey and paler underneath.

The only historical reference that may refer to this species is that of 3 toothless whales killed about 1839 near Eynhallow, and mentioned by Baikie and Heddle. They were each about 5m in length. There have been 6 confirmed strandings :

- 1933 17th Jun 1, Burwick, South Ronaldsay, 4.8m
- 1954 29th Apr 1 male, North Ronaldsay, 4.7m
- 1961 19th Jun 2 females, Birsay, 4.8m and 3.4m
- 1999 19th Apr 1, freshly dead at Helzie, near Rapness, Westray, 4.57m
- 2000 23th Mar 1, not fresh, near Knap of Howar, Papa Westray, c4.5m. Part of the beak was missing, the skull is in the National Museum of Scotland, Edinburgh
- 2001 25th Jul 1 which has been dead some time, St Catherine Bay, Stronsay, 3.96m

## PORPOISES : Phocoenidae

### HARBOUR PORPOISE *Phocoena phocoena*

Common

Photo ©Chris Booth

Predominantly a coastal species found mainly in shallow water over the Continental Shelf.

The harbour porpoise has a short robust body with a rounded head and a small, centrally placed, triangular dorsal fin. Females are slightly larger than males, with an adult length of 1.4-1.6m. Upper parts are dark grey in colour, lighter on the sides; the underside is white. There are 38-56 small spade shaped teeth in the upper and lower jaws. The harbour porpoise surfaces with a rolling motion showing just the dorsal fin and part of the back. It rarely breaches.

This species is the smallest and most numerous cetacean to be seen around Orkney. It was described by writers in the 19th century as common in summer and autumn, although Baikie and Heddle also stated that none were seen in winter. Whether there has been any change in status is difficult to say but, since regular recording began, it has been noted throughout the year. It is certainly much commoner from June to September with July and August being the peak months and is least often reported in February and March.

Monthly distribution of sightings - 1980-2004

| J | F | M | A | M | J | J | A | S | O | N | D |
|---|---|---|---|---|---|---|---|---|---|---|---|
| 29 | 15 | 19 | 53 | 96 | 169 | 262 | 280 | 152 | 80 | 45 | 27 |

It seems to favour the more sheltered waters, the area to the south of Scapa Flow between Cantick Head and South Ronaldsay often holding the largest numbers. Sightings have varied from 1 to over 100 but those of 1-6 are most common, although groups of 10-15 are not infrequent.

Strandings have occurred throughout the year with no obvious peak months. 2 freshly dead juveniles, with umbelical cords still attached, have been found on the 4th and 7th June in 2 separate years, they measured 80cm and 81cm respectively. This probably indicates that the harbour porpoise gives birth in Orkney waters and also shows the time of year when the calves are born. A female stranded near Burray on 18th September 1993 measured 1.73m and is one of the largest ever recorded in Scotland.

## DOLPHINS : Delphinidae

### SHORT-BEAKED COMMON DOLPHIN *Delphinus delphis*

Formerly rare; commoner in recent years

Worldwide distribution, common in the north east Atlantic.

A small slender dolphin with a long beak and centrally placed dorsal fin. Length 1.8-2.4m, males being larger than females. Grey-black on the upper side with a distinctive hourglass pattern on the sides which has a yellowish colouration in front of the dorsal fin and whiter behind. There is a dark triangle below the dorsal fin. There are approximately 40 small pointed teeth on either side of upper and lower jaws. A very active dolphin, a fast swimmer, often breaching.

There are no historical records of this species, the first definite report was of 1 stranded in December 1921. Up until 1994 there are records of a further 8 strandings, 1 each of 3 and 2 dolphins, the rest of singles and just 1 sighting . It has become more frequent in the last 10 years, although it must still be considered uncommon. There were 2 sightings between 1994 and 2002, with schools of 5 and 6 in June and July. Several records in 2003, with 6 in Widewall Bay, South Ronaldsay on 21st May, 5 spent some time around a sea angling boat off the West Mainland on 19th July. On this date a school of between 20 and 40 appeared in Scapa Flow and were present there until at least 24th July, putting on spectacular breaching displays. On 26th May 2004 between 30 and 50 were present for about 2 hours on the west side of No.1 Barrier and were watched by many people.

There have been 6 strandings, all of single dolphins, which have occurred between 1994 and 2004. Of these 2 were juveniles, 1 of which was a new born female, length 95cm and weighing 9.4kg, found at Evie, Mainland on 12th July 2000. As this was freshly dead it must have been born in Orkney waters

Monthly distribution of strandings - 1921-2004

| J | F | M | A | M | J | J | A | S | O | N | D |
|---|---|---|---|---|---|---|---|---|---|---|---|
| 1 | 2 | 2 | 3 | 1 | 2 | 1 | 0 | 0 | 0 | 0 | 3 |

## STRIPED DOLPHIN or Euphrosyne Dolphin *Stenella coeruleoalba* Very rare

Worldwide distribution in tropical, sub-tropical and warm temperate waters. Common in the Mediterranean and off the Iberian peninsula.

Photo: Chris Booth

A small dolphin, similar in size and shape to the common dolphin, with a long slender beak and sickle shaped dorsal fin. Dark grey on the upper side with a distinctive light grey patch on the sides of the body extending from the eye up to the dorsal fin. Also on the sides are 2 blackish lines, 1 running from the eye to the flipper and the other from the eye to the underside near the tail. There are 40-50 small pointed teeth on either side of the upper and lower jaws. A very active dolphin, often breaches.

This species is fairly new to the Orkney list. There have been 3 strandings, all of single dolphins :

- 1997 14th Sept Sower, Orphir Mainland, reasonably fresh. Length 1.77m
- 1998 20th Mar Birsay, Mainland, dead some time. Length 1.70m

The skulls of both dolphins are in the National Museum for Scotland, Edinburgh

- 2004 31st March Scapa Beach, a juvenile which stranded alive but died. Length 1m

## BOTTLE-NOSED DOLPHIN *Tursiops truncatus* Rare

Worldwide distribution in tropical and temperate seas. There is a resident population in the Moray Firth.

A large robust dolphin, 2-4m in length, with no definite markings. Grey on the upper side becoming lighter underneath, with a distinct beak and a fairly tall, slender, sickle-shaped centrally placed dorsal fin. There are 18-26 teeth on either side of the upper and lower jaws. A very active dolphin, it often breaches and performs acrobatics. This is the dolphin most commonly seen in dolphinariums and in films.

- The only historical reference is of a male and female, both 2.6m in length, that stranded alive at Swanbister Bay, Orphir in September 1888.

It is possible that this species occurs more regularly around Orkney, particularly in the Pentland Firth, than records suggest.

Sightings :

- 1987 8th Nov 8+ seen 10 miles east of Sule Skerry and 3+ seen 25 miles west of Kirkwall

Both sightings were made from an aircraft en route to North Rona

- 1994 15th Oct 1 Pentland Firth
- 2001 11th Jan 5 Pentland Firth
- 2002 12th Aug 2 or 3 off Rora Head, Hoy
- 2003 18th Jun 5 off North Ronaldsay

The only stranding of this species is of 1, which was found in an advanced state of decomposition, on 24th July 1988 on Egilsay, length 2.6m.

## ATLANTIC WHITE-SIDED DOLPHIN *Lagenorhynchus acutus* Uncommon

**(Flaked or flecked whale)**

Photo © P & V Reynolds

Confined to the northern North Atlantic and mainly found in offshore waters.

A large robust dolphin, 2-2.8m in length with a short beak and thick tail stock. The dorsal fin, which is tall and sickle shaped, is centrally placed. The upper side is black with a long oval blaze on the flanks, the anterior part of which is white, but yellow ochre towards the tail. There are 58-80 teeth in the upper and lower jaws. An active dolphin which breaches, but bow-rides less often than does the white-beaked dolphin.

The white-sided dolphin was considered by Buckley and Harvie-Brown to be "not rare" in the 19th century. They mentioned that it was called "Flaked or Flecked whale" and, if present amongst a herd of pilot whales, made them difficult to drive. It is common over the Continental Shelf to the northwest of Orkney but is less often seen in the coastal waters around the islands than the white-beaked and Risso's dolphins.

The largest school reported was between 50 and 100 near Sule Skerry on 31st October 1976. Most other sightings have been of 2-8 dolphins but 30-40 were present in St Mary's Bay, Scapa Flow on 23rd July 2000.

Monthly distribution of sightings - 1976-2004

| J | F | M | A | M | J | J | A | S | O | N | D |
|---|---|---|---|---|---|---|---|---|---|---|---|
| 0 | 0 | 0 | 1 | 1 | 0 | 2 | 5 | 1 | 1 | 1 | 0 |

Strandings of 1-3 animals have occurred throughout the year, with slightly fewer in the summer. Of the stranded dolphins that were measured 5 were between 1.4m and 1.85m in length and 14 from 2.04-2.7m showing that both immature and adults have been involved.

Monthly distribution of strandings - 1970-2004

| J | F | M | A | M | J | J | A | S | O | N | D |
|---|---|---|---|---|---|---|---|---|---|---|---|
| 0 | 2 | 2 | 3 | 2 | 0 | 1 | 1 | 1 | 1 | 4 | 1 |

Apart from the above, of 7 that stranded at Scapa on 12th May 1994, 6 were rescued. 1 that stranded on 27th July 1994 was moved into deeper water and swam away strongly.

## WHITE-BEAKED DOLPHIN *Lagenorhynchus albirostris*

Formerly fairly common, now uncommon

Confined to the northern North Atlantic but more often found in coastal waters than the white-sided dolphin.

A large stout dolphin, very similar to the previous species, with a short beak which is often white in colour. It is black on the back with a pale grey area behind the large, centrally placed sickle-shaped dorsal fin, forming a saddle. This pale area extends on to the flanks, the belly is white. There are 45-56 teeth in the upper and lower jaws; these teeth are larger than in the white-sided dolphin. A very active dolphin which breaches and bow-rides.

There is only one 19th century record, that of a group of 7 or 8 seen at Longhope, Hoy on 28th June 1853. This was claimed by Buckley and Harvie-Brown to be the first record for Orkney. The next report was not until 1953, when 1 stranded at the Bay of Deepdale, Holm. Whether the lack of records in the 19th and early 20th century is a true reflection of the scarcity of this species during this period is now difficult to say.

Since 1980 it has been one of the commonest dolphins reported in Orkney waters but the number of annual sightings has definitely declined in the last 10 years. It has been most frequently seen from July to October with an obvious peak in August. Many of the sightings have been off the west coast of Orkney.

Monthly distribution of sightings - 1980-2004

| J | F | M | A | M | J | J | A | S | O | N | D |
|---|---|---|---|---|---|---|---|---|---|---|---|
| 0 | 0 | 2 | 2 | 2 | 3 | 12 | 27 | 13 | 4 | 0 | 0 |

Most sightings have been of 1-6 dolphins but there have been single reports of schools of 15 and 20-30.

Strandings have occurred throughout the year and, on several occasions when the dolphins have still been alive, it has been possible to move them into deeper water.

The majority of strandings have been of single dolphins, but there have been four strandings of 2 and one of 3 animals. Both juvenile and adult dolphins have been involved and of those that have been measured, 6 were from 1.18-1.40m in length and 15 from 2-2.92m. From the sightings and strandings of both live and freshly dead animals it would seem that white-beaked dolphins may be present in all months around our coasts.

## KILLER WHALE *Orcinus orca*

Fairly common in recent years

Worldwide distribution. Found in both northern and southern hemispheres from polar to tropical seas.

Striking black and white markings with a distinctive white oval patch above and behind the eye and a pale grey saddle behind the dorsal fin. The belly and throat are white. The centrally placed dorsal fin in adult males is tall and triangular and in females and immatures is sickle shaped. The flippers are paddle shaped. Length 5-9m with adult males being considerably

larger than females. There are 10-13 teeth on both sides of upper and lower jaws.

The killer whale appears to have been fairly common in both the 18th and 19th centuries, according to the historical writers. Unfortunately there is no information for the 20th century until the late 1970's. From 1979-1990 it was recorded in 9 of these years, with the number of annual sightings ranging from 1-8. Since 1992 it has been recorded annually with numbers increasing since 1998 and an exceptional number of reports in 2003 and 2004. Sightings have occurred throughout the year but it has been most commonly seen from May to September, with an obvious peak in July which coincides with the time that common seal pups are present.

Monthly sightings - 1979-2004

| J | F | M | A | M | J | J | A | S | O | N | D |
|---|---|---|---|---|---|---|---|---|---|---|---|
| 1 | 3 | 4 | 4 | 12 | 42 | 59 | 22 | 8 | 3 | 1 | 2 |

Numbers seen have ranged from 1-20 but most sightings have been of 5-8 animals, although 10-17 have been reported on at least 17 occasions. Many pods have contained at least 1 adult male and in some 1-3 juveniles have been present. Frequently the sightings have occurred in the vicinity of common seal haul-outs and there have been several accounts of them attacking seals. The whales have also been observed feeding on shoaling fish and on one occasion attacked a flock of moulting eider ducks. There have only been 3 strandings, all of single animals, since 1977.

## LONG-FINNED PILOT WHALE *Globicephala melas*
**(Bottle-nose, Caa'ing whale)**

Formerly common, now uncommon

Photo - Mass stranding, Mill Bay, Eday ©P & V Reynolds

Photo © P & V Reynolds

Usually a deep water species although it does come into coastal waters. Found mainly on the edge of the Continental Shelf to the north of Scotland and southeast of the Faroe Islands, also from southern Ireland south to the Bay of Biscay.

Length 4-6m with a bulbous rounded head. The dorsal fin is set well forward on the body, is flag shaped in the male and broad sickle shaped in the female. The flippers are long and slender, the body black in colour with a lighter underbelly. Spy hops, when the body stays vertical with head above the water.

This species has been exploited in Orkney in the past as a source of food, when herds of these whales were driven ashore. One of the earliest mentions of a drive is by Wallace in 1693, who reported that 114 had been driven ashore in 1691. In the 19th century there are records of at least 8 drives between 1834 and 1889. The number of whales killed ranged from 50 to at least 450, the latter drive occuring on Westray in the autumn of 1843.

It was certainly common in the 19th century as Baikie and Heddle mentioned that it appeared in Orkney in herds of 50 to upwards of 500. However, the account by Moodie-Heddle in Buckley and Harvie-Brown, that he once saw Scapa Flow full, "many thousands extending for miles", should be treated with caution!

There are no records of either sightings or strandings in the first half of the 20th century, this may be due to the lack of recording rather than the absence of whales. There were 5 mass strandings in the second half of the 20th century :

- 1950 22th Apr 96 Stronsay
- 1955 14th Mar 67 Point of Cott, Westray, 54% females
- 1983 12th May 36 Twiness, Westray, 62% females
- 1983 16th Dec 28 Mill Bay, Eday, 64% females. Lengths of 8 males varied from 3.64-6.30m and of 14 females from 2.36-5.46m
- 1986 20th Dec 18 Bay of Stove, Sanday, 5 died and 13 were rescued

Sightings were regular between 1980 and 1993 and involved herds of up to 80 whales. They were seen most frequently between May and August.

Monthly distribution of sightings - 1980-1993

| J | F | M | A | M | J | J | A | S | O | N | D |
|---|---|---|---|---|---|---|---|---|---|---|---|
| 0 | 0 | 1 | 1 | 3 | 4 | 3 | 3 | 1 | 0 | 1 | 1 |

Strandings for the same period, unlike sightings, were commoner from October through to January

Monthly distribution of strandings - 1980-1993

| J | F | M | A | M | J | J | A | S | O | N | D |
|---|---|---|---|---|---|---|---|---|---|---|---|
| 6 | 0 | 2 | 0 | 2 | 1 | 0 | 0 | 0 | 2 | 2 | 3 |

Since 1993 there appears to be have been a definite change in status and the pilot whale is now, at least, uncommon. From 1994 to 2004 there have only been 9 sightings, all between April and October and involving 1-12 whales. In the same period, there have been 8 strandings, all of single whales, 5 occurring between July and September and the other 2 in February and November.

## RISSO'S DOLPHIN *Grampus griseus*

Regular, fairly common in August

Photo ©Drew Kennedy

Photo ©Pete Reynolds

Found in tropical and temperate waters worldwide. The northern limit of their range in the eastern Atlantic is around Shetland and off Norway.

A large, robust dolphin 3.3-3.8m in length, the males are slightly larger than the females. It has a rounded head and a large centrally placed sickle shaped dorsal fin which can be darker in colour than the body. The body is greyish in colour, lightening with age to become almost white. The numerous scratch-like markings over the body may be present from birth. There are usually 4 peg-shaped teeth on each side in the lower jaw with none in the upper jaw. This is a fairly active dolphin, it breaches and tail slaps, also spy-hops.

The Risso's dolphin is not specifically mentioned by historical writers, which may have been due to the difficulty in recognising the different dolphin species. The first definite record is that of 1 stranded in November 1933 and there are a further 11 stranding incidents recorded up until 1980. The only sighting in this period was of 4 off Lamb Holm in March 1973. Since 1980 it has been recorded more regularly than any other dolphin species. It is seen most frequently from June to October with August and September the peak months for sightings.

Monthly distribution of sightings - 1980-2004

| J | F | M | A | M | J | J | A | S | O | N | D |
|---|---|---|---|---|---|---|---|---|---|---|---|
| 0 | 0 | 0 | 2 | 1 | 4 | 3 | 28 | 24 | 10 | 2 | 0 |

The maximum school size reported has been 20, the majority of sightings have been between 3 and 8 dolphins but a minimum of 10 have been recorded on at least 4 occasions. Juveniles have been noted between July and September.

Despite the lack of sightings in mid-winter, strandings have been more evenly distributed throughout the year.

Monthly distribution of strandings - 1980-2004

| J | F | M | A | M | J | J | A | S | O | N | D |
|---|---|---|---|---|---|---|---|---|---|---|---|
| 2 | 2 | 2 | 1 | 1 | 0 | 4 | 1 | 1 | 2 | 4 | 2 |

On 3 occasions dolphins that have live-stranded have been moved into deeper water with apparent success. Lengths of stranded dolphins have ranged from 2.44-3.5m.

## WHALE & DOLPHIN WATCHING

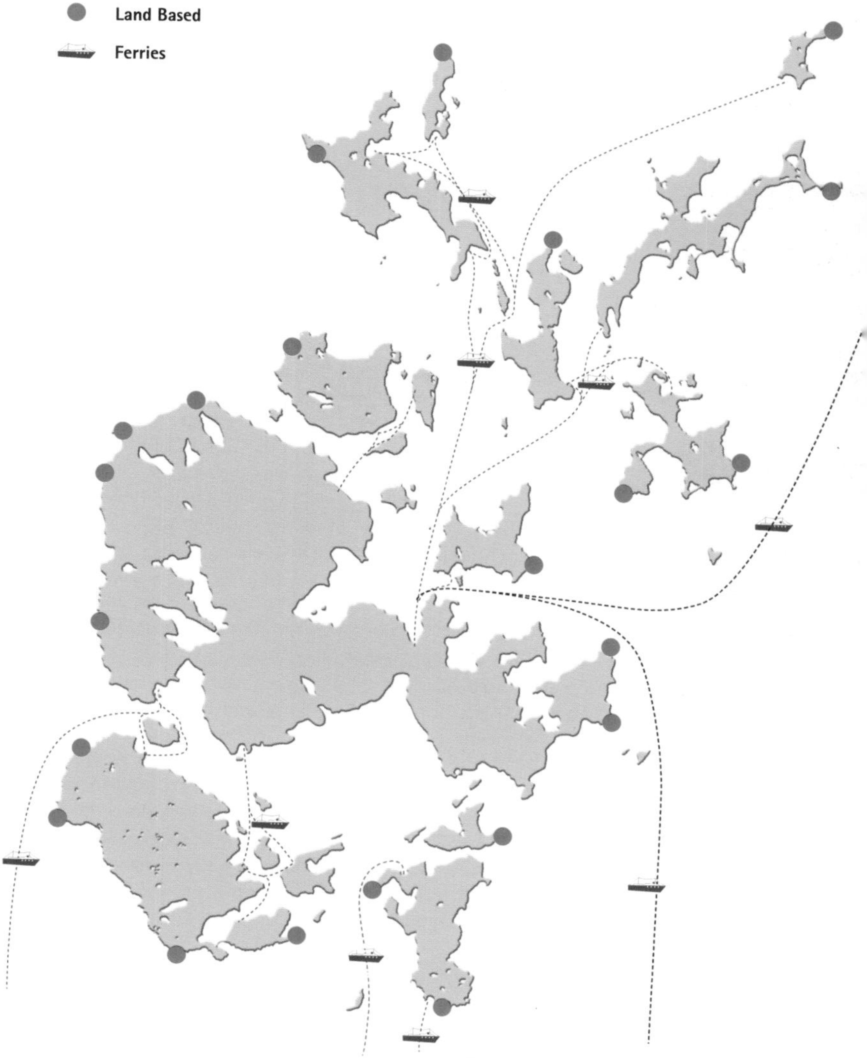

## TERRESTRIAL CARNIVORES : Order Carnivora

### Mustelidae

**FERRET** *Mustela furo* — Introduced

In 1999 about 12 of these animals were released on Stronsay in a misguided attempt to reduce the rabbit population. The majority had been recaptured by April 2000 and the ferret does not appear to have become established on the island.

Apart from the above, there have been occasional reports of animals that have escaped from captivity.

**OTTER** *Lutra lutra* — Fairly common

Photo ©Rod Thorne

Found throughout Europe, range restricted now in many areas including mainland Britain.

The otter has an elongated body with short legs, a flat head and a broad muzzle with obvious whiskers. It has a long tapering tail and webbed feet with five toes on each foot, dark brown fur, a paler throat and sometimes white under the chin. Body length 60-70cm, tail 39-45cms and the weight is 7-10kg.

The otter probably arrived in Orkney before the first human settlers. It has definitely been established for many centuries and remains of otters have been found at archaeological sites. It was considered to be common in the 18th and 19th centuries and, although there may have been a slight decline, it is still widely distributed and fairly common throughout the islands. One of the limiting factors in its distribution may be the lack of suitable holt sites.

In Orkney, the otter may not be as easily watched during the day as it can in parts of Western Scotland and in Shetland. Even so, otters are reported regularly from some of the North Isles such as Eday, Sanday and Westray and can also be seen in the less disturbed areas of the larger lochs on Mainland. It is probably best observed during the early morning and at dusk.

Signs of otter activity are most obvious in the vicinity of burns which run down onto beaches and sheltered coasts. In the past, hunting may have posed a threat, however at present the main dangers appear to be from deaths on the road and accidental drowning in creels. Of the 106 reported deaths between 1979 and 2004, 70 were killed on the road, 14 drowned in creels, 8 from disease or injury and 14 from causes unknown. These figures are probably biased towards road deaths as they are the most obvious, but there is anecdotal evidence to suggest that many accidental drownings in creels are not reported.

Analyses of spraints have shown that the fish most frequently taken are five-bearded rockling, bull-rout/sea scorpion, saithe and eel. Mammal remains, including those of common rat, amphibian bones and feathers have also been found. Otters have been seen attacking domestic ducks and also eating a freshly dead rabbit and a goldeneye, but it is not known whether these had actually been killed by the otter.

### CATS : Felidae

**FERAL CAT** *Felis catus* — Common

Feral cats appear to be well distributed throughout all the larger inhabited islands of Orkney and are especially in evidence along the edges of cliffs, in rough grassland and moorland areas. Often associated with rabbit warrens they will quickly disappear down a burrow when disturbed.

Judging by the numbers of small mammals, especially voles, and also birds that fall prey to domestic cats, the impact of the feral ones on Orkney's wildlife must be quite considerable.

Litters of small kittens have been seen from June through to October. The feral cat population is probably being continually augmented from straying and abandoned domestic cats.

## SEALS ETC : Order Pinnipedia

### SEALS : Phocidae

Seals have been hunted in Orkney for centuries, not only for their skins, but also for oil and for food. The small island of the Barrel of Butter, in Scapa Flow, apparently got its name from the rent paid by the people of Orphir for the right to kill seals there in medieval times. Buckley and Harvie-Brown mentioned an account, written by Pitcairn in 1787, of an annual trip to Sule Skerry where he had seen from 500 to 1,000 seals caught in about 48 hours. Seals were also netted on skerries in both the North and the South Isles.

Apart from the common and grey seal, 4 vagrant species of seal have been recorded in Orkney.

**COMMON SEAL (Selkie, Tang-fish)** *Phoca vitulina* Very common

Widely distributed around the shores of northern oceans.

Colour variable, black grey or light brown often spotted with light and dark markings. When dry it can appear almost white. The head has a dog-like appearance, rounded at the top with nostrils at a "V" angle. Length 120-160cms, weight 100-130kgs.

This species appears to have been abundant in the 19th century but, because the very early historical writers did not distinguish between common and grey seals, it is not possible to comment on its earlier status. It still remains abundant although there can be fluctuations in numbers at different haul out sites, this is sometimes influenced by local disturbance. Largest numbers of the common seal can be found in sheltered waters and around undisturbed coasts where there are suitable haul-out sites such as northeast Mainland, the islands of Scapa Flow, Stronsay, Sanday and Westray.

# Mammals

Photo ©Rod Thorne

In Orkney the pups are born in June and early July, they are active just after birth and are able to swim as soon as water covers the rocks on which they were born.

Common seals can enter the Loch of Stenness by swimming under the Brig o' Waithe and are regularly seen hauled out on rocks near the Standing Stones, usually 1-4 but up to 14 have been recorded. Occasionally they haul out near Voy, approximately 4.5kms from the outflow, the furthest distance from the sea in Orkney that a common seal can reach by swimming.

● Location of some haul out sites of common seal

## GREY SEAL (Selkie, Haaf fish) *Halichoerus grypus*

Very common

Found on both sides of the Atlantic extending up into the Arctic.

Photo ©Rod Thorne

Variable in colour, often dark grey with paler areas and spots which are often larger and less numerous than in the common seal. It has a large head and elongated muzzle which gives a Roman nose appearance, with the nostrils separated at the base and almost parallel. Adult males are much larger than females, the length of the males being 207cms and weight 230kg, and the females 180cm and weight 150kg.

The grey seal was not common in Orkney, according to Buckley and Harvie-Brown, writing in 1891. There were signs of an increase at the end of the 19th century, continuing into the 20th century. They were first reported around the Green Holms in about 1930 and the population increased significantly from then on. The restriction on hunting and less disturbance at breeding grounds, especially when some of the smaller islands became depopulated, may have been one of the contributing factors.

Numbers of grey seals increase greatly in autumn as they congregate on their breeding grounds, which are mainly on small uninhabited islands, particularly around the Westray Firth and the southern approaches to Scapa Flow. Breeding also takes place on sheltered beaches on islands such as South Ronaldsay, and pups may be found on any relatively undisturbed stretch of coast where the cows are able to haul out.

● Location of some of the main breeding areas of the grey seal

Cow seals come ashore from late September continuing throughout October and pups are born from the end of September, with a peak period in late October and early November. The last pups leave the beaches in late December.

## RINGED SEAL *Phoca hispida*

Very rare

Common in the Arctic around icebound coasts, also found in the Baltic and the Caspian Sea.

A small seal, 140cm in length and weighing 65-95kg. It has a pale grey ground colour with a number of black spots which are surrounded by ring-shaped lighter markings, particularly on the back. Underside is silvery grey.

There is a probable reference to this species by Baikie and Heddle, who mentioned a rough or bristled seal *Phoca hispida*, 1 or 2 specimens of which had been obtained.

- The only definite record is of an exhausted juvenile found at the Mill, Tankerness on 31st July 1992. It had moved up the burn from the sea to the mill pond where it was annoying the local farmhouse ducks! It was taken into care and, fully recovered, was released at Deerness on 26th August.

## HARP SEAL *Phoca groenlandica*

Very rare

A migratory species found in the extreme northern parts of the North Atlantic.

Highly migratory, it breeds in the spring on the pack ice and in summer moves into the open waters of the Arctic Atlantic.

The sexes are similar in size with a length of about 170cm and a weight of 130kg.

The adult male is grey with a dark face and a black band over the neck and extending back along the flanks. The female is browner, the dark markings often being broken up into spots.

The only records are from the 19th century :

- 1 was shot several years prior to 1848.

A female and young were seen near the Galt Skerry, Shapinsay. Unfortunately the year is not known and there is now no way of checking the authenticity of this record.

## BEARDED SEAL *Erignathus barbatus*

Very rare

Found in shallow coastal waters of the Arctic, this species feeds mainly on molluscs and is not usually migratory.

The most obvious feature is the large number of long whiskers on the upper lip. Colour usually grey with a brownish tinge about the head. A large seal 2.2-2.7m in length, it can weigh up to 260kg.

There are just 4 records :

- On 24th April 1987 an adult was seen in Deerness, this was probably the same seal that had been seen in Shetland a few weeks earlier.
- In 1988 a juvenile approximately 1.5m in length was reported from several areas between February and 23rd July. On 16th May it came into Kirkwall Harbour and hauled out on the Corn Slip. It was very tame and allowed a close approach.

- On 29th August 2004 a juvenile, about 1.5 metres in length, appeared in Kirkwall Harbour. This also hauled out on the Corn Slip and like the previous individual it was very tame.
- One, approximately 2 metres in length, hauled out at The Ouse, Finstown on 29th March 2005. It stayed in the area for about 3 weeks.

## HOODED SEAL *Cystophora cristata*

Very rare

Found in Arctic regions of the Atlantic, often on drifting ice, this species apparently occurs regularly in Faroese waters.

Photo ©Ross Flett

The males are larger than the females, with a length of up to 2.5m and weight of 400kg. Adult males have an enlargement of the nasal cavity which forms an inflatable crest or hood on top of the head. Grey in colour, lighter on the sides and underneath, with irregular darker markings over the body. The pups have a distinctive coat which is slate grey on the back and white underneath.

There is an historical record of an adult shot and another seen in November 1890 on Sanday. More recently there are 3 records of juvenile seals :

- A male was found dead on the east side of Glimps Holm on 12th August 1998, it was just over 1m in length.
- In 1999 a male hauled out on the Corn Slip in Kirkwall Harbour on 21st January. It was taken into care but died later and was found to be undernourished. It had a length of 1.2m and weighed 23kg.
- On 20th September 1999 a female was found alive on the beach at Echnaloch Bay, Burray but died the next day. It had a weight of 39kgs.

WALRUS : Odobenidae

## WALRUS *Odobenus rosmarus*

Very rare

Found in shallow waters around Arctic coasts.

A very large animal, the adult males can be up to 3.6m in length and weigh over 1,200kg, the females are smaller. Compared to the body, the head is small and adults have 2 large tusks. The skin, which is wrinkled in appearance, varies from greyish to reddish in colour.

There are several 19th century records but, as whaling ships calling in at Orkney ports occasionally brought young walruses back from the Arctic, their provenance is uncertain.

- The only confirmed recent record is of one seen ashore on the Point of Grory, Eynhallow on 4th August 1986. The observers commented on the large size, presence of tusks and the skin, which had cracks and was pinkish in colour.

# UNGULATES

HORSE, CATTLE, SHEEP : Order Artiodactyla

CATTLE, GOATS, SHEEP : Bovidae

## SWONA CATTLE *Bos taurus*

When the island of Swona was evacuated in 1974, a herd of cattle was left behind. Supplementary feed was given up to 1977 and in this year some of the cattle were removed. Since then the herd has remained unattended.

Derived from Shorthorn and Aberdeen Angus stock there were 33 animals in 1985 and just 15 in 1995. In July 2004 18 animals were counted and these were either black, brown or white in colour.

Apart from the Chillingham herd in Northumberland the Swona cattle are the only other herd of feral cattle in Britain.

## NORTH RONALDSAY SHEEP *Ovis aries*

North Ronaldsay sheep are a breed of Northern short tailed primitive sheep, related to the Soay sheep of St Kilda and the primitive sheep of Iceland and Scandinavia.

Photo – North Ronaldsay sheep feeding on the shore © Chris Booth

This breed is small and horned, the ewes weigh about 13.5kg. The fleeces come in a variety of colours, grey being the commonest.

On North Ronaldsay they are confined to the shore by a stone wall which runs around the perimeter of the island, thus keeping them away from the cultivated land. Here they feed mainly on seaweed as there is only a limited area of rough grazing available to them.

In Orkney, as well as being found on North Ronaldsay, they have recently been introduced into Linga Holm and Auskerry.

# References

**GENERAL**

BAIKIE and HEDDLE. 1848. Historia Orcadensis Part 1. Edinburgh.

BUCKLEY, T.E. and HARVIE-BROWN, J.A. 1891. A Vertebrate Fauna of the Orkney Islands. David Douglas, Edinburgh.

BOOTH, CHRIS and JEAN. 1998. Status and Checklist of the Vertebrate Fauna of Orkney. Kirkwall.

GROUNDWATER, W. 1974. Birds and Mammals of Orkney. Kirkwall Press.

LOW, Rev. G. 1813. Fauna Orcadensis. Published and edited by W. Leach, Edinburgh.

**FISH**

BOOTH, C. 1997. The list of fishes collated by the Orkney recorder in Scotland's Biodiversity : Challenges and Opportunities. ICIT, Heriot-Watt University, Orkney.

BOOTH, C.J. Fish records 1998-2004 In Orkney Field Club Bulletins 1999-2005.

BOOTH, C.J. 2000. The Stone Loach in Orkney. Glasgow Naturalist 2000 Volume 23 Part 5: 57.

DAY, F. 1880-1884. The Fishes of Great Britain and Ireland. London and Edinburgh, 2 vols.

ICES. 1993. Atlas of North Sea Fishes. ICES Co-operative Research Report No. 194. International Council for the Exploration of the Sea, Copenhagen.

NELSON, J.S. 1984. Fishes of the World (2nd Edition). John Wiley, New York, (3rd edition, 1994).

SANSOM, B. 1999. List of fishes from inter-tidal and shallow sub-tidal areas on Egilsay. Orkney Field Club Bulletin 1999 : 44-45.

SIDE, J. 1997. The Biodiversity of Orkney Fishes in Scotland's Biodiversity : Challenges and Opportunities. ICIT, Heriot-Watt University, Orkney.

SIDE, J. 1998. Fishes. Unpublished paper presented to a workshop on Orkney's Marine Biodiversity at the Orkney Science Festival, September 1998.

SIDE, JONATHAN. 1998. Orkney Fishes and some absentees from the recent local record. Orkney Field Club Bulletin 1998 : 18-20.

SIDE, J. 1999. Montagu's sea snail / Nilsson's pipefish. Orkney Field Club Bulletin 1999:36.

SIDE, JONATHAN. 2000. A Preliminary Survey of Flatfish Nursery Grounds. Orkney Field Club Bulletin 2000 : 50-52

SIDE, JONATHAN. 2000. Weever Fishes. Orkney Field Club Bulletin 2000 : 52-53.

WHEELER, A. 1978. Key to the Fishes of Northern Europe. Frederick Warne, London.

WHEELER, A. 1992. A List of the Common and Scientific Names of Fishes of the British Isles. Journal of Fish Biology, 41 (Supplement A).

**AMPHIBIANS AND REPTILES**

Records up to 1993 have been summarised in Booth and Booth 1994.

BOOTH, CHRIS and JEAN. 1994. Amphibians and Reptiles, appendix in The Mammals of Orkney. Kirkwall. pages 42-48.

BOOTH, C. J. Amphibian and Reptile records 1994-2004. In Orkney Field Club Bulletins 1995-2005.

**BIRDS**

Records up to 1982 have been summarised in Booth, Cuthbert and Reynolds 1984, since then in the annual Orkney Bird Reports 1983-2004.

# References

BOOTH, C, CUTHBERT, M and REYNOLDS, P. 1984 The Birds of Orkney. The Orkney Press, Kirkwall.

LLOYD, CLARE, TASKER, MARK L. and PARTRIDGE, KEN. 1991. The Status of Seabirds in Britain and Ireland. T & A.D. Poyser London.

MITCHELL, P.I., NEWTON, S.F., RATCLIFFE, N. and DUNN, T.E. 2004. Seabird populations of Britain and Ireland. T. & A.D.Poyser London.

ORKNEY BIRD REPORTS 1974-2004.

TAY and ORKNEY RINGING GROUPS. 1984. The Shore-birds of the Orkney Islands. Perth. Tay Ringing Group.

WILLIAMS, E.J. 2000. Wintering Seafowl in Scapa Flow, Orkney, October 1998 to March 1999. Scottish Birds 21 : 15 - 26.

**MAMMALS**

Records up to 1993 have been summarised in Booth and Booth 1994.

BOOTH, CHRIS and JEAN. 1994 The Mammals of Orkney. Kirkwall.

BOOTH, CHRIS and JEAN. 1994 The Mountain Hare in Hoy. Orkney Field Club Bulletin 1996 : 42.

BOOTH, C.J. Bat records 1994-2004. In Orkney Field Club Bulletins 1995-2005.

BOOTH C.J. 2001. Diet of the Otter. Orkney Field Club Bulletin 2001:16.

CORBET, GORDON B. and HARRIS, STEPHEN. (Eds) 1991. The Handbook of British Mammals. (3rd ed). Blackwell Scientific Publications, Oxford.

COSGRAVE, P. 1999. Rat colonisation on Eynhallow. Orkney Field Club Bulletin 1999:16.

ORKNEY CETACEAN REPORTS. 1994-2004. Booth, C. J. (Ed). In Orkney Field Club Bulletins 1995-2005.

SPENCE, SHEILA. Mammal records. Orkney Field Club Bulletins 1995 : 52, 1998 : 28 and 1999 : 38.

## Fish

# Index



## Amphibians

# Index

## Reptiles



## Birds

# Index

# Index

# Index

## Mammals

# Index